Praise for

MY MIND IS NOT ALWAYS MY FRIEND

"Wise advice, clearly presented, on how to lead a more fulfilling life."

HELEN ASTIN, PHD, AND ALEXANDER ASTIN, PHD,
PSYCHOLOGISTS, DISTINGUISHED PROFESSORS EMERITI,
UCLA GRADUATE SCHOOL OF EDUCATION
AND INFORMATION STUDIES

"Steve incorporates sound psychological concepts into a very creative and inspiring read!"

—WALTER E. BRACKELMANNS, MD

"Parents who use Steve Fogel's guidance for living a more fulfilling life will not only reap enormous personal benefit, they will also be role models for their children in ways that promise them a brighter future."

ANN PLESHETTE MURPHY,
AUTHOR, *THE 7 STAGES OF MOTHERHOOD*,
AND PARENTING CONTRIBUTOR, *GOOD MORNING AMERICA*

"As a psychiatrist, I found Steve Fogel's book to be a deeply honest and realistic guide to help you recognize how you think, feel, and behave and how the problems you face today are rooted in your past. It's also a useful tool that can assist you in making necessary changes to improve your experience of life."

DIANE WEISS, MD

"Steve's book is a game changer. His insights will improve your life."

GRAY DAVIS,
FORMER GOVERNOR OF CALIFORNIA

"Steve Fogel dissects and examines the human decision-making process and the mental barriers that prevent us from flourishing—personally and professionally. In *My Mind Is Not Always My Friend*, he outlines the importance of awareness and commitment to overcoming self-destructive, self-defeating behavior. His book is a dynamic tool to help individuals understand and adjust patterns that prevent them from being fully present and productive. Becoming aware of our individual 'programming' and using Steve's exercises to engage in active reprogramming of ourselves and our responses is crucial to achieving goals and to overcoming subconscious obstacles in our mental processes. Steve's book is highly readable and an important read for us all."

STUART GABRIEL,
DIRECTOR, ZIMAN CENTER FOR REAL ESTATE,
UCLA, AND ARDEN REALTY CHAIR AND PROFESSOR OF FINANCE,
UCLA ANDERSON SCHOOL OF MANAGEMENT

"I suggest you take a deep breath and dive into this book. Fogel's hard-earned wisdom could transform your life. This book will help you put those debilitating inner voices to rest so you can reach your creative potential."

RUTH WEISBERG, DEAN,
USC ROSKI SCHOOL OF FINE ARTS

"Engagingly written and deeply thought provoking. Fogel has a winning style and insightful perspective on how the mind works for us—and sometimes against us. A fascinating work."

CONGRESSMAN ADAM SCHIFF

"This book is both interesting and educational. It is a fast read and a profitable experience."

RABBI ISAIAH ZELDIN

My Mind Is Not Always My Friend

A Guide For How To Not Get In Your Own Way

Steven J. Fogel

with Mark Bruce Rosin

FRESH RIVER PRESS
Los Angeles, California

The excerpt on pages 166-7 is from the book *The Four Agreements* © 1997, Miguel Angel Ruiz, M.D. Reprinted by permission of Amber-Allen Publishing, Inc. P.O. Box 6657, San Rafael, CA 94903. All rights reserved.

Fresh River Press
Tel: (310) 820-5443 www.mymindisnotmyfriend.com

Ordering Information

Quantity sales/orders for college textbook/course adoption use. Special discounts are available on quantity purchases by corporations, associations, and others. For details, contact the "Special Sales Department."

Orders by U.S. trade bookstores and wholesalers. Please contact BCH: (800) 431-1579 or visit www.bookch.com for details.

Printed in the United States of America

Cataloging-in-Publication Data

Fogel, Steven Jay, 1942-.

My mind is not always my friend : a guide for how to not get in your own way / by Steven Jay Fogel ; with Mark Bruce Rosin.

p. cm.

ISBN 978-0-9845525-3-5

Includes index.

1. Self-actualization (Psychology). 2. Success. 3. Peace of mind. 4. Conduct of life. 5. Behavior modification. I. Rosin, Mark Bruce. II. Title.

BF637.S4 .F62 2010

158.1--dc2222   Library of Congress Control Number: 2010927257

First Edition

15 14 13 12 11 10   10 9 8 7 6 5 4 3 2 1

Acknowledgments

I would like to thank Dr. Neil Haas, Dr. Robin Kay, Dr. Ron Levine, Dr. Leana Melat, Rabbi David Woznica, EST, and Landmark Education for helping me break free to live a better, more fulfilling life; Mark Bruce Rosin, my lifelong friend and coauthor, for his invaluable contribution to this book; Michael Levin and Brookes Nohlgren for their editorial and production help; and Victoria Trevino for her love, support, and wisdom.

CONTENTS ✦

YOUR WORST ENEMY CANNOT
HARM YOU AS MUCH AS YOUR
OWN UNGUARDED THOUGHTS.

SHAKYAMUNI BUDDHA

I AM NOT WHAT HAPPENED TO ME.
I AM WHAT I CHOOSE TO BECOME.

CARL JUNG

PREFACE

Do you run your mind…or does your mind run you?

Is it possible to have everything you ever wanted…and still wonder if this is all there is?

Your computer and your cell phone know what day it is; is your mind still living in the past?

I've spent decades working through these questions. If they also resonate with you, then we have a lot in common. I have written this book to offer my insight into resolving these issues… so that you can live right here, right now, and be satisfied with your life while growing spiritually.

In his classic book *As a Man Thinketh*, James Allen wrote, "Man is made or unmade by himself; in the armory of thought he forges the weapons by which he destroys himself; he also fashions the tools with which he builds for himself heavenly mansions of joy and strength and peace."[1]

In the privacy of your own mind, what are you creating for yourself?

1

My career has been in the field of commercial real estate, so perhaps the metaphor of building heavenly mansions of thought is especially appealing to me. This book is a blueprint to show you how you can examine your thinking, and change it where it's not serving you, because your thoughts are the building blocks of the life you desire.

My partner and I started our real estate investment company in 1969 with a 24-unit apartment house in Los Angeles. Today our company has grown into a billion-dollar-plus portfolio of shopping centers across the United States. As a result of our success, many people have sought me out for mentoring, both in business and their personal life, wanting to learn the concepts, tools, and techniques that have helped me get where I am today.

Invariably these people start out with the belief that wealth is going to be their ticket to happiness. Being rich is supposed to relieve stress and provide the ability to concentrate on living instead of making a living. It's true that being rich certainly relieves the stress people face if they cannot pay their bills, and this is especially apparent in times of economic hardship. But that's not the only expectation we have about the power of money. We believe that being rich will provide not only an affluent lifestyle and social prominence but also the answers to all our problems. That's why we believe being rich will make us happy.

I used to believe this, too. My family was lower middle class, I put myself through college in the early '60s, and I set the goal of becoming a millionaire by the time I was 30. I achieved my objective and was proud of my success, living the lifestyle I'd dreamed of and having professional recognition. I had a talent for both making and keeping money. But surprisingly—at least surprisingly to me—the happiness this gave me was fleeting. I soon found that the old line "Money can't buy happiness" was true—and the joke was on me!

At 26, I had a lovely home, a wife, and, soon, kids. At 36,

I came home to a true Hollywood mansion, a picture-perfect family, and all the things I'd thought I was supposed to have. I was outgoing, good with jokes and stories, and usually had a smile on my face, but no matter how much I accomplished— how much I had—inside I never truly felt good for long. I was still trapped in the same feelings of frustration and suffering that I'd experienced since childhood, and wealth and all it bought me didn't help me escape.

For the past 35 years, I've been searching for answers to the psychological and spiritual mysteries of life. I've been in therapy, participated in human potential workshops, read books on self-help and spiritual teachings, and enjoyed a full physical fitness life. I engaged in all the methods for self-transformation that came across my path, hoping to find the antidotes to my emotional pain.

Along the way, in addition to running my company, I became a painter, a writer, took up music, acting, stand-up comedy, and produced a few small movies. I had fun expressing my creative side and applying the lessons I'd learned about self-transformation.

I was experiencing more joy, but I still felt incomplete. I started to realize that what was missing was a sense of purpose to my life. Then, after many years of searching for it, my purpose came to me: I feel I've been called to share my life lessons, to teach the self-transformation techniques I've learned on my search, in order to help others relieve unnecessary pain and get out of their self-imposed straightjackets.

This book is my opportunity to share what I've learned about experiencing emotional freedom: the freedom to be in the present, the freedom to feel joy, the freedom *just to feel*.

You may have already heard the words immortalized by Ram Dass: "Be here now." Though Ram Dass's book by that title was published in 1971, it took me over three decades to fully understand why "being here now" is so important, not just intellectually but through my own experience.

What I've learned is that we as human beings can only feel peace—in fact, feel our true feelings, which is what allows us to experience peace—if we are in the present, and most of us are rarely in the present!

The reason for this is that although we're unconscious of it, many of us are controlled much of the time by how we've interpreted and responded to events in our past. These interpretations and responses created patterns of thinking and behavior that we get locked into. They keep us in the past while simultaneously projecting us into the "what ifs?" of the future. If we are stuck in the past (which is gone) or projecting into the future (which hasn't happened yet), we cannot be in the present, and yet we are only fully alive in the present.

Why would we continue to be controlled by our past and project ourselves into the future if living this way prevents us from being fully alive? And what can we do to change this?

The answer to these questions is the subject of this book, and it starts with the phrase "although we're unconscious of it." Most of us simply don't recognize that we're rarely in the present.

Before I began to see this, I thought I was in the present all the time. I didn't realize that my mind's internal dialogue—the voice in my head that comments on everything I do and experience—was running all the circumstances and relationships in my life and that it was running them based on interpretations I had made of events in my past that, unconsciously, I was still carrying around with me.

I had no idea that the stress, anxiety, and frustration I experienced in relationships was all due to unconsciously living in the past or to projecting myself into the future and that there really was no problem in the present other than that it didn't always fit my pictures of how my life was "supposed to be"!

We all want to be happy 24/7, and yet we have an endless list of things we think must be different before we can be happy: We need the right job, the right relationship, or we need to solve our problems with our parents, siblings, or children. We don't realize that the real reason we aren't happy is internal, not external. As I'll share with you, I came to see that not only were my patterns of behavior based on my past experiences, those same factors were causing me to act in ways that made my future just like my past. My past was automatically running, and in some areas running away with, my life.

Most of us allow our old patterns to control our lives, and we don't have a clue that it is happening. We hear the voice in our head constantly evaluating ourselves and others and every circumstance we encounter, making judgments that tell us what to do or not do, but we don't realize that what it's telling us is based on our past and not always accurate.

Some experiences—like pride in our achievements or enjoyment of another person—can be pleasurable because they match our mind's expectations or pictures of how things "should" be, and our internal dialogue comments, "Wow, that's great!" Other experiences—like someone we're attracted to not being interested in us—run smack up against something that our mind tells us is a threat to getting what we want, and the voice in our head begins to worry.

This happens because the perception of being threatened catapults us, on an unconscious level, back to threats we experienced long ago and activates the feelings we associated with them. Chronologically we are in the present but we are flooded with feelings from the past. The anxiety we feel prevents us from effectively responding to the present. This anxiety is not in response to the present—to what's happening here now—but to our past, or to our future (which we think will be determined by our current situation).

This is how our past controls our current actions and reactions and, as a result, sets the table for our vision of the future. Often we're unconscious that the future hasn't actually happened yet. We behave as if we know exactly what the future will be. When this happens, we are setting up our future to look like our past, with little potential for aliveness and joy.

Impulsiveness, quickness to anger or hurt, cutting off emotionally, or allowing ourselves to be taken advantage of by others out of fear of confrontation are common examples of recurring behaviors that we fall into because we are controlled by our past and not living in the present. In fact, behaving in a certain way again and again even though it doesn't help us lead a fulfilling life is a sign that we're not living in the present, and a sign that we are not opening ourselves to the potential for aliveness and joy. As you read this, can you think of any repetitive behavior of your own that sabotages your efforts to lead the life you want?

Therapy 101 teaches that the definition of insanity is doing the same action over and over and expecting a different outcome. Yet most of us do this every day. Fortunately, we can do something about our unconscious, patterned ways of thinking and behaving so they don't have so much power over us. Instead of living in the past and letting it determine our future, we can use the strategies in this book to bring ourselves into the present and create a future with far more possibilities than we've ever imagined.

All of us are growing, just not at the same speed and not starting at the same place. Transformation can come in the blink of an eye, though for most of us it doesn't. Usually we are so set in our ways that, unless we experience a severe physical or emotional shock that acts like an earthquake to shatter our ingrained patterns, we rarely do what is necessary to rebuild ourselves psychologically and change our behavior to truly make a difference in our experience of life.

We resist change through our defenses, unconscious mechanisms that block us from the feelings and thoughts our conscious mind is unable to cope with. Our defenses keep us from seeing truths and acting on them. They keep us stuck, no matter how much we tell ourselves we would like to change.

For years my defenses kept me feeling like I was emotionally handicapped, as if other people had a broader range of feelings than I did. I silently felt I had been shortchanged in the emotions department. Through my searching I came to recognize that my defenses were preventing me from connecting with other people and their feelings. Intellectually I had empathy; emotionally I felt out of touch. I believed that was just how it was. I didn't know that it was possible for me to shed my defenses and open up and feel. But I have found that I can, and today my life is richer and my relationships far better because of it.

The transformation of the caterpillar into the butterfly only comes when it comes; until then, the caterpillar is a caterpillar. We all have an enormous potential for good feelings, but we can only experience joy when we learn how to interrupt the unconscious patterns of thinking and behaving that prevent us from being in the present. Until then, we stay stuck. My goal in this book is to help others improve the quality of their lives by sharing what I've learned on my journey, which allows me to be more alive at 65 than I was at 25.

In the business world, we talk about business management skills—techniques that can help to prevent or resolve problems and produce positive outcomes. I think of the lessons I've learned and am going to share with you as life management skills. They provide a blueprint for how to identify and manage behavior that up 'til now has been disruptive to the life you would like to lead. This book can't heal you—you can only do that experientially, usually with the guidance of a trained therapist who can help you learn to feel the feelings you have unconsciously repressed through your defenses—but this book will teach you techniques to help you get through the maze of life with less self-destructive behavior and more aliveness, and it will help you lay the foundation for healing and make suggestions for how you can do it.

PART 1
THE MIND:

MACHINERY VERSUS

CONSCIOUS CHOICE

CHAPTER ONE
CREATION OF THE MIND AS WE KNOW IT

The Garden of Eden

I believe that there is a Source, a Higher Power, a force that connects all to all and that is inside each and every one of us. The Old Testament contains archetypal stories about the human condition, which, I believe, provide mythology that our psyches need, giving us insights that help us to understand ourselves.

Genesis, the beginning of the Old Testament, tells the story of the Garden of Eden. Initially, everything was perfect in the Garden of Eden. There was absolutely nothing to be concerned about; in fact, the concept of "concern" didn't even exist, because there was complete harmony.

When God created Adam and Eve, they were part of this harmony. He told them about two trees in Eden: the Tree of Life and the Tree of Knowing and Not Knowing, also called the Tree of Knowledge. God instructed Adam and Eve that they must not eat any fruit from the Tree of Knowledge. When God created them, Adam and Eve experienced themselves and everything around them as unjudged, unfiltered experiencing. They were perfect and their lives were perfect. They had no problems and survival wasn't an issue. They were immortal; nothing could do them harm. They had no fear and no defenses.

If they had followed God's instructions, they could have stayed this way for all eternity. But the well-known snake came into Eden and enticed Eve to disobey God and eat a fruit from the Tree of Knowledge, and Eve tempted Adam to eat the fruit, too. Once they tasted this forbidden fruit, God sent them out of the Garden of Eden with the instruction to "go forth and multiply," and they were no longer immortal. They would live and die, and they experienced a tentativeness about existence that they had never known before. They were now worried about survival.

As I interpret the story, it was at this moment that the mind as we know it came into being to help Adam and Eve and their descendants, the human race—us—to survive. The mind started reacting to the outside world, which now contained threats, since there was no longer total harmony. The voice that they each now had in their heads started making judgments, telling Adam and Eve what to do and what not to do for their survival. It gave them information about how to act, just as today it gives us information about how to act.

The sages of Eastern philosophy consider enlightenment to be getting rid of that voice—transcending the mind. For most of us, the mind and its voice are operating in this mode 24/7, judging and scanning everything with the intended purpose of keeping us safe.

Before the creation of the judging mind, when Adam and Eve were experiencing life unfiltered and unjudged, they were experiencing what I think of as pure beingness. The harmony that prevailed in Eden meant that they were always fully present in the present, always connected to the Source—the Higher Power—to each other, and to the entire world. Time did not exist; everything was eternal.

Once they ate the fruit and the mind as we know it came into existence, every time that voice spoke to them judgingly they were cut off from pure beingness, from the sense of total harmony. Suddenly there was a future to worry about, a present with potential threats to survive so that they could live into the future. There was also a past that the mind began to use as a reference point to see what worked for them and what didn't, and to apply its inferences from these past experiences to help them survive the present and think about the future.

After Adam and Eve left the Garden of Eden, God instructed them to go out and multiply, and multiply they did. As time passed, we humans formed small groups of 30 or 40 and lived in tribes. In the time of the woolly mammoths, it took a tribe of this size to survive. We were hunters and gatherers back then and needed to travel in packs to stay alive. It was critical not to be ostracized by the rest of the pack, because being shunned was a death sentence.

Building on the programming that the human mind had constructed since leaving Eden, our minds now learned to program our behavior so that we would be compatible with the pack. This was about 2.5 million years ago. In terms of its programming, the human mind hasn't run on the same technological clock as modern science. Our minds have helped us develop many scientific advances, but in some respects, such as our need to fit in with the pack, there has been little in the way of evolution. In many ways our mind is programmed the same way today as it was in prehistoric times.

When our mind is operating automatically with patterned responses, I will refer to the workings of the mind as our machinery and to the "software" that determines our responses as our programming.

In the next chapters, I'm going to explain in detail what I've come to understand about how the workings of our mind play out in our lives. I'm also going to explain how knowing this helps us see clearly why our initial response to a situation is sometimes self-defeating, and how we can learn to respond in a different, more fulfilling way.

Pause Your Machinery

Here, and in many of the chapters that follow, I'll ask you to stop and take a moment to "pause your machinery." The concepts I present in this book all require some practice and mindfulness, so these brief exercises will give you the opportunity to stop, step outside of the usual pattern of reading passively, and bring yourself into the present moment to reflect on your life, see how the information you've just learned applies to you, and integrate what you can from it.

Before going on and examining in depth how our programming turns into actions, I'd like you to Pause Your Machinery.

- Take out a pen and paper and list two or three incidents in your life that did not work out the way you would have liked. These can pertain to love, family, work, or any other area. Don't think about it for too long; just choose incidents from your past that were significant enough to quickly come to mind now.

- Start with the first incident and pretend it is a scene in a movie being projected on the screen of your mind. Watch the scene, then write a brief description of what occurred, being sure to include your thoughts about it, how it made you feel, how you acted and reacted, as well as what the other people involved did or said. Repeat this step for each of the incidents you have chosen.

- Next, re-create each incident in your mind, only this time describe what happened without making any judgments about it—that is, leaving out your thoughts and emotional reactions. In other words, write down just the facts, without interpreting them as "good" or "bad," or interpreting them to mean something about you as a person, your life, your future, another person, or people or life in general. Again, this time, just the facts of what occurred.

- Compare your descriptions of each incident. Can you see how your interpretation of the events has affected their significance to you?

Save this list of incidents, your description of them with your thoughts and feelings, and your description of them with just the facts. And keep it handy: I will ask you to refer to it later, at the end of the book.

CHAPTER TWO

THE MIND'S MACHINERY AND AWARENESS

There is a continuing debate about biological versus environmental influences on our emotional development: nature versus nurture. The biological is our DNA, the genetic makeup we are born with; the environmental is our physical surroundings, including Mom and Dad and the messages they download to us. Our mind's machinery automatically uses everything we hear, see, and sense to write and rewrite our basic programming, which continues to get more and more sophisticated throughout our lives.

All of this programming is written based on our interpretations of what we've experienced. As a kid, I was told shrimps and crabs were scavengers, not clean, and not good to eat. I wrote that into my child's culinary database. Later in life, I had to rewrite that programming when I found out that with the proper cocktail sauce they were tasty (especially cracked crab with mustard and mayonnaise)! On the other hand, I got frightened the first time I went to the dentist because he poked me with scary tools, and although no dentist has hurt me for years, I still get nervous in the dental chair due to that original childhood experience. For some reason, my machinery was willing to rewrite my interpretation of shellfish but, so far, not my interpretation of the dentist.

The voice in our head that comes from our machinery takes our judgments and interpretations and turns them into stories or tales, which it replays over and over. They become the basis of our programming, which forms the patterns of our behavior. How we experience life varies for each of us depending on the past experiences we've had, starting in the womb, and on our interpretations and reactions to those experiences.

The machinery uses that programming from early childhood to react over and over to what happens in the present. These reactions are very predictable, with one exception: Every once in a while, for no real reason, the machinery will react differently. This is what makes us so interesting. We react the same way, the same way, and the same way—and then we react differently to the same situation and we think, "Wow! I've grown!" and then, amazingly, we go back to the old pattern. This is part of the human condition; we are always predictable except when we're not—but what is predictable is that when we're run by our programming, much of the time we respond in the same old ways.

Remember, in the Garden of Eden there was no need for programming. God created Eden to be harmonious and Adam and Eve as experiencing pure beingness. Everything changed when we ate the forbidden fruit and had to leave Eden. Then, for the first time, we had free choice. Our machinery started out with a blank canvas. God was no longer the author; it was up to us. In effect, we were now gods in our own unique universe when it came to providing each detail of our unique world.

In some ways, each of our universes is like a fingerprint: It is different from all others in specific details because it is personally programmed through our unique interpretations of our individual experiences. Our machinery builds stories around our relationships and a million other things we encounter in our lives.

These tales are intended to ensure our survival and, as part of that survival, our place in the tribe to protect us from woolly mammoths. As I'll show you in the following chapters, much of our stress and anxiety comes from our worries—conscious and unconscious—about survival and the stories we make up in connection with it.

However, here's the vital point: We don't have to allow our mind's machinery to run us; our mind has another capacity, too—the capacity to become aware of how the machinery works and to learn how to interrupt it and make conscious choices. To use this ability, which we all have, we must do two things:

1. We have to make the commitment to become aware of how the machinery works.
2. We have to back up this commitment with our will to transform ourselves so that we remain aware and interrupt our machinery in order to make conscious choices.

Awareness, without the will to use it to transform ourselves, is not enough. When we do not use our conscious mind to interrupt our machinery, our machinery's programming determines how we experience every moment of every day, and we experience these moments as the same as, or similar to, moments from our past and we act accordingly, which is often not in our best interest. This is why the stakes are so high for us to learn exactly how our machinery works and why it's important to interrupt it when it's producing self-defeating behavior.

Pause Your Machinery

Write your responses to the following:

- Identify an association—good or bad—from your child-hood, like my aversion to dentists.
- Describe instances when this childhood association has colored your perception of an otherwise unremarkable activity, event, or place.
- In what ways has this association influenced your behavior? For example: causing you to put off the dental appointment you know you need, or to hesitate to order the shellfish your friends encourage you to try.

Take a moment to come up with ideas about what you could do the next time this feeling comes up to notice it and choose a different behavior or response. List your ideas.

CHAPTER THREE

WHAT OUR MIND'S MACHINERY TELLS US IN EARLY CHILDHOOD AND HOW IT CAN CONTROL US TODAY

We are born with no limitation on communicating our feelings and thoughts. A young child speaks without censoring him- or herself, but then something happens and we begin suppressing ourselves; instead of communicating our feelings and thoughts as they occur, we begin holding back.

The "something" that happens is an event that we experience as an emotional trauma. Observed from outside, the event can be large—a death or divorce—or seemingly small—a parental reaction of irritation to something we've done—but even an event that looks small from the outside can be emotionally traumatic for a child. How we react to this trauma and to subsequent traumas establishes patterns of behavior that we tend to unconsciously allow to determine our behavior as we react to new events.

True growth starts when we realize that our actions are being triggered by an event that activates old patterns of behavior and we begin to understand which old patterns are being triggered by which particular external catalysts. The key is mindfulness—the mind's ability to stay conscious—so that we can be aware of how and when our machinery gets triggered. This means that we have to see and understand the ways our machinery reacted to past traumas and the programming that formed at that time, which is still with us.

Our programming is a combination of very old pre-bundled software inherited at birth from our species' woolly mammoth days mixed with our new childhood interpretations of the specific events of our young lives.

The traumas that form our programming vary for each of us, but they all share a common dynamic: An event occurs and we interpret the event to mean that "there is a terrible problem and it has to do with me."

I remember being a preschooler and my dad coming into the living room and finding his high school yearbook on the floor. He quickly discovered that I had used his treasured possession as my coloring book and had scribbled all over it. In my child's mind, he went ballistic. I got scared and interpreted this incident to mean that I was bad, very bad.

But what actually happened? He was angry and I was frightened by that anger and I felt cut off from his love. To my child's machinery, I could be screamed out of the Garden of Eden for the cardinal offense of coloring. The 2.5-million-year-old part of my preprogrammed child's machinery kicked in. Without a clue, I was right back in the Woolly Mammoth Age of hunting and gathering, and I was afraid of being banished from my previously secure childhood. My dad, leader of my woolly mammoth-hunting tribe, is mad at me, really mad, and he may want to punish me. My unconscious interpretation was, "You'll be out of the tribe!"—a potential death sentence. The message that entered my programming from that day forward was, "You better be super good and never do anything wrong so that you'll be safe!"

Los Angeles therapist Dr. Robin L. Kay describes the most common childhood trauma as "ruptures of an emotional attachment." In the incident I related, I experienced my father's anger as a rupture in our attachment bond. The parent-child bond is generally the most important emotional attachment in childhood. We need our parents' love in order to feel safe, and if we experience a rupture it is traumatic.

According to Dr. Kay, when the rupture of an attachment bond occurs, it can be repaired in real time soon after the event by the person with whom the rupture occurred, thereby helping the child to resolve the trauma. Research suggests that only 50 percent of ruptures between parents and children need to be repaired to lead to "good enough" parenting of a child, meaning that the child will generally have a positive self-image and function well enough in the world, behaving in ways that are in harmony with his or her goals. In other words, the more times we have someone able to help us repair traumas when we're children, the less negative programming we have as adults.

When parents are able to repair a rupture with their children, they are helping their children learn to use this same process to build the needed infrastructures for resolving traumas in the future on their own. Thus, as Dr. Kay puts it, "effective co-regulation leads to effective self-regulation": When parents process and repair the hurt (or anger or any other feelings) that creates a rupture with their children, not only is that rupture repaired but the children are also developing their own emotional-processing kit for later in life.

When a trauma is not quickly repaired, not only does a child feel pain from the trauma, but soon other emotions also become layered on top of the pain: rage at the parent (using my example), guilt for being enraged at him, grief over what the child believes is the loss of his father's love, and longing for his father to love him. These layered feelings can be called complex feelings. If the trauma remains unrepaired, these complex feelings stay with us and we may not be aware of them. Often they are repressed and defended against, so we remain blocked from fully experiencing them because our conscious mind finds them unacceptable or intolerable.

When the machinery interprets and stores information that is negative and that causes dysfunctional behavior in the present, it's because the programming was formed from a trauma that was not repaired. As we develop in childhood and become more sophisticated, our negative interpretations become four basic ideas:

1. There is a terrible problem here. (*Here meaning everywhere.*)
2. I'm flawed.
3. I don't fit in.
4. I'm doomed to be on my own.

There's no way to avoid this programming if, as children, we've had many unrepaired ruptures in emotional attachment to our parents or to others we loved and needed, or if we've had large ruptures caused by particularly traumatic events. It's how our machinery works in childhood and continues to work throughout our lives, controlling us until we learn to interrupt it.

As I've mentioned, our mind's machinery is constantly scanning everything we experience and producing judgments and evaluations of it, and for most of us this becomes an almost constant voice in our heads. Some of the information the machinery gives us is productive and helpful. In fact, we could not survive without the mind's machinery. On the most fundamental level, the mind's machinery helps us to avoid physical jeopardy. For example, it may automatically tell us to look before we cross the street so that we won't be run over by a car or to slow down if we're driving on a dangerous winding road.

But many of the machinery's judgments and evaluations actually prevent us from getting what we truly desire. This may seem contradictory: If the mind's machinery is there to help us survive, and we want to have harmonious and healthy relationships and an enjoyable life, why does it give us information that creates frustration, stress, and anxiety? Why does it give us information that prevents us from reaching our goals? Why does our own machinery sabotage us? That sounds crazy!

The Machinery and Survival

To understand how our machinery interprets what will be good for our survival, we have to look in more detail at how it works.

Every experience we've ever had is monitored by our machinery and filed away for future reference. An event happens—say, somebody looks at us a certain way that the machinery questions and perceives as a "strange look." The look happens during an ordinary conversation, and we keep the conversation going while our machinery does an instant search of what that "strange look" meant. It comes up with a file (memory) that seems to apply to the look, and the voice in our head instructs us accordingly, even though that "bit" of information—the machinery's interpretation of the look as disapproving of us—may send us in the wrong direction, perhaps for the rest of our lives.

With so many "bits" being reviewed in real time, it's no wonder that the machinery often applies a piece of information that looks like it fits a current circumstance but that turns out to be the wrong piece of information, retrieved from a file of a past situation, that is really not applicable to the present moment.

Another way of saying this is that the machinery uses past experience as its operating manual, and when it misjudges the present situation as similar to an earlier event that it interpreted as a threat, the machinery uses the past strategy even though it is not the appropriate tool for this new situation. This results in poor instructions that can backfire.

Unlike an appropriate strategy that we can learn from the past, such as, "Fire is hot! Don't touch the stove again when it's on," dysfunctional strategies—based on our misinterpretations and on our defenses (our patterns of dealing with or avoiding our emotions)—work against us, keeping us from being fully alive.

Later we'll look more closely at defenses. The point I want to make here is that because of misinterpretations and inappropriate associations, the machinery's programming often functions as though it is responding to an actual threat when in fact our survival is not being threatened. When this happens, the machinery kidnaps our being—that fundamental part of ourselves that is capable of living in the here and now—and takes us out of the present and starts giving commands. The voice in our head is now on full battle alert. I call this "being activated."

When we are activated, our actions are working on automatic pilot and we have stopped being objective. In the example of the person giving us the "strange look," once the machinery has interpreted the look negatively, it sends out rapid-fire judgments and evaluations, and we become ready to fight, run, manage, manipulate, charm, or act in a dozen other possible ways to deal with this new threat. And it's only a look that our machinery perceives as a threat to our survival!

We could have interpreted that same look as the other person saying, "You're cute," or "You're ugly," or "You're dangerous." Depending on how we've interpreted it, we get flattered or embarrassed or angry; we open ourselves up to the other person, or we run, or we shut down from fear of rejection or fear of closeness. The list of possible interpretations and actions is endless.

Once the machinery becomes activated, if we do not make a conscious choice to interrupt it and consciously say to ourselves, "Stop! This isn't going to work for me!" and to ask ourselves, "What is really happening? What interpretations have I added to it?" the machinery takes over and we are no longer in the present. The machinery has taken complete control of what we say and do in the outer world.

When our mind is on automatic pilot while we're driving and it keeps us at the proper speed limit, stopping for stop signs and red lights, responding appropriately to other drivers, then our mind is keeping us safe. If our mind is on automatic pilot but is being activated by our old programming that results in inappropriate or self-destructive behavior, then we can clearly benefit by becoming conscious of what is activating our programming and learning to interrupt it.

For me the most frequent activation comes from a situation in which I feel I'm being "shamed" or "blamed." It's as if the shame or blame is a filthy slime that has been thrown at me. It drives me crazy. My inner world feels like it might explode if I don't get it off instantly. The perceived shame or blame brings me right back to the childhood experience of my father's anger when he found his defiled high school annual. Those four basic ideas I held—"There's a terrible problem here," "I'm flawed," "I don't fit in," and "I'm doomed to be on my own"—are instantly front and center in my activated machinery, and it becomes an emotional emergency, perhaps a minor emergency, but a problem that must be dealt with.

My whole sense of self-worth goes temporarily out of order. My inner world can't stand to see myself like that; it's too painful. I have to vindicate myself immediately. I have no choice! I start using automatics, old tapes that successfully fought off similar problems earlier in my life. It's like my mind has a library of these tapes and intuitively selects one without even considering if it's actually the correct one, let alone the appropriate response to the situation. More often than not I become defensive without even being aware of it. These automatics are like old ghosts that come back to life when I'm on automatic pilot.

Let's say I'm having a conversation with a friend and everything is fine. All of a sudden he says something that my mind interprets to mean, "Steve, you're wrong, you don't understand." My mind tells me I'm being shamed and blamed. I feel covered with disgusting slime and I feel like I need to do something quickly or I will be annihilated. In short, I'm activated!

I'm not aware that my machinery is activated and that I'm responding as though my life is actually being threatened. All I know is that I can't allow him to say that I don't understand. My mind isn't really listening anymore. My machinery has to destroy the concept "I don't understand," which it interprets as my friend saying I'm a jerk, which my machinery believes is an attack to be defended against, and I have to counterattack the other person. At that point, I'm no longer in the present. I can't hear what he's saying because I'm reacting on automatic pilot to the perception that I'm being shamed and blamed, which my mind's machinery interprets as being threatened, and thus my survival must be protected.

From its point of view, my machinery is just defending my survival, because "You don't understand" (its interpretation of my friend's comment) means that I'm "stupid" or "incompetent," which I fear will make my tribe consider me to be putting them at risk against the woolly mammoth, and therefore they could throw me out and I wouldn't survive alone. (This is the underlying fear behind the beliefs that "There is a terrible problem here" and "I don't fit in.")

Of course it doesn't occur to me that my friend may not have meant what my machinery interpreted him to have meant. When my machinery is activated, it is driving me, and its only objective is to eliminate the threat at all costs, whether the threat is real or imagined. This is what happens until my machinery gets out of the driver's seat and my being becomes present. *The mind's machinery wants to keep the being that holds the life force from being killed, but in the process it blocks the experience of beingness—it blocks our ability to feel our true feelings; it blocks our sense of connectedness to the Higher Power.*

When the machinery takes over, we may have feelings of love, longing, anger, grief, and guilt, or we may experience an internal conflict or a heightened state of "fight or flight" or "engage or disengage." Often our emotions become exaggerated and distorted or we become anxious. The key point is that when our machinery is running us, what we are feeling is determined by our programming and its interpretations of current situations based on past experiences.

Our machinery's programming is filled with defenses that cause us to unconsciously repress many feelings, and we don't have a clue that we're doing it. Our machinery judges these feelings to be too explosive for us to handle, so we hide them from ourselves and we unconsciously stuff them down and just feel anxiety instead of our true feelings.

Sometimes our machinery causes us to feel intense feelings as a distorted reaction to a present event. As we've seen, these feelings are not in response to the current event but rather to our unconscious misinterpretation of the event as being similar to a past event (or, more accurately, to our interpretation of that past event). Our machinery can also cause us to have a distorted emotional response when we consciously think about a past event if our programming contains a misinterpretation of that event.

However, when we learn to interrupt our machinery and become conscious in the present and aware of our programming's misinterpretations, our feelings are no longer being automatically programmed by our machinery. It's only then that we feel appropriate, authentic feeling responses in the present.

Pause Your Machinery

Write your responses to the following:

- Identify and briefly describe an instance in the recent past when your programming reacted as if your survival was being threatened and you felt a sudden surge of anger, defensiveness, or shame in reaction to something someone else said or did. Your example can be as simple as a flareup of your temper in a slow-moving line at the grocery store, or it can be an incident with further-reaching connotations, such as your feeling angry, defensive, or ashamed in response to your boss during a performance review or in a heated disagreement with your spouse.

- As you envision the scenario, isolate in your mind's eye the specific look, words, behavior, or circumstance that first set off your programming's survival response. Summarize what the catalyst or trigger for your survival response was.
- Do you see a connection between your response and one of the four common underlying beliefs discussed in this chapter: "There's a terrible problem here," "I'm flawed," "I don't fit in," or "I'm doomed to be on my own"? If so, name the belief and describe how it triggered you to respond with anger, defensiveness, or shame.
- Are there other recent instances you can easily think of where this core belief also triggered your programming? If so, describe the incidents and their relationship to the belief.

The mind's machinery never allows us to just be. The voice in our head is always judging and evaluating, telling us what to say, what to do. It is not only activating feelings but also commenting on them. Our machinery is trying to control everything—even though the effort is futile—and it becomes frustrated and stressed when it has to confront the fact that it has failed, once again, to control what it wants to.

This is why we are not fully present when our machinery is running us. By contrast, when the machinery is interrupted, we can get back to that place of just being. We are fully present, we experience a connection to ourselves, to the full range of our true feelings. We are capable of being at peace. We can experience a connectedness to the Higher Power. I think of this as being the Self, with a capital "S," in contrast to the self, with a small "s." The self with a small "s" is the "I" and the "me" that we think of as ourselves, but actually this self is our machinery's perception of ourselves.

When we interrupt our machinery, we are simply being, and

whatever we are feeling is perfect because it just is. When we are just being, our machinery is hibernating and we can be in touch with our intuition. We are living in the moment.

CHAPTER FOUR

THE JACK STORY:
HOW THE MACHINERY'S INTERPRETATIONS
CAN MAKE US ACT DISRUPTIVELY

I once had the opportunity to interview a world-renowned architect about his career. One of the major points he wanted to talk about was how he overcame his self-destructive behavior to achieve his success. He told me "The Jack Story" to explain the negative way his machinery often operated before he learned to interrupt it.

In this fable, long before cell phones, a man rents a car that gets a flat tire in the middle of the night while he's driving through a blizzard in a remote location. The man has no choice but to fix the tire immediately or potentially freeze during the long night. He goes to the trunk of the car and finds that there's a tire but there's no jack, so he decides to walk to a farmhouse and borrow one.

As he trudges through the heavy snow to the farmhouse, his mind starts imagining what's going to happen. It starts out with nice thoughts, but eventually he starts fantasizing that the farmer will mistake him for the classic killer in a horror film who approaches the lonely farmhouse with a story so that he can get inside. The man's fantasy escalates to the point of imagining that upon opening the door, the farmer will be pointing a gun at him instead of being kind and lending him the jack. By the time he gets to the house and the farmer opens the door, the man is so angry from imagining the worst that he says to the stunned farmer, "To hell with you and keep your goddamned jack!"

The architect told the story to illustrate how his negative programming had always so prepared him for a fight with clients that he had started fights when there was no necessity for them. With the help of a therapist he had become aware of this pattern and learned to identify it and stop it from occurring.

Whenever we allow our negative programming to run us, we lose all of our power. When the mind's machinery kidnaps the being and commandeers the driver's seat, it is going to make us go where it wants us to go, regardless of any future negative impact.

When my son was small, he got hit in the face by another child. My son told his karate instructor about it, and the instructor asked him if he hit the other boy back. "No," my son said, "he was my friend." The karate instructor responded, "No, he wasn't your friend. A friend wouldn't do that to you." This is why I say *my mind is not always my friend.* My son's mind got in the way of his self-protection. His machinery misidentified the other child as his friend and used the label "friend" to deny the child's hostile action toward him. My son's machinery mistakenly saw the other child's "friendship" as being important for his survival rather than identifying the other child as an actual threat.

Our mind's programming to do what it thinks is best for us is based on earlier programming that, as we've begun to see, may not fit the present situation. My favorite metaphor for the mind's machinery is HAL, the computer in the film *2001: A Space Odyssey.* In the next chapter, I'll show you how HAL applies to us.

CHAPTER FIVE

CONFLICTING MISSIONS:
WHY OUR MACHINERY'S PROGRAMMING FOR SURVIVAL IS NOT ALWAYS BEST FOR OUR BEING

2001: A Space Odyssey is a classic sci-fi movie from 1968. Written and directed by Stanley Kubrick, the film deals with elements of human evolution, technology, and artificial intelligence. The storyline centers on a multiyear space journey that starts out with five astronauts on a sophisticated spacecraft. HAL, the onboard supercomputer—which I liken to our mind with its machinery and the voice in our head (indeed, HAL has a voice and speaks)—is programmed to assist the astronauts in every aspect necessary to accomplish their mission.

For a while everything goes perfectly, but eventually the air supply is cut off for three hibernating astronauts. The two conscious astronauts realize that HAL is responsible for the other astronauts' deaths. The surviving astronauts plan to disconnect HAL, but HAL overhears them and decides it must kill them first. It almost succeeds. Fortunately, one astronaut survives and enters HAL's "Logic Memory Center." As HAL futilely attempts to negotiate with the astronaut, we, the audience, see HAL slowly regress to past memories and finally fall silent.

In the film's sequel, *2010,* scientists find more information about the first journey when they retrieve the spacecraft and reactivate HAL. A psychologist asks HAL why it acted as it did, and the computer lets the psychologist know that in killing the astronauts it was working entirely in accord with its programming. Its programming demanded that above all else the spacecraft was to arrive at its final destination, and HAL judged the astronauts' actions as threatening that objective.

This parallels what often happens when we allow our machinery to run us. Unless we learn to interrupt our mind's machinery and make conscious choices, our machinery, acting on what it believes is best for its mission of survival, makes our lives dysfunctional— just as HAL's attempt to take over the mission was dysfunctional (to say the least) for the astronauts. Our machinery's programming may not kill us, but in fulfilling its objective of doing what it interprets as needed for our survival it often kills our aliveness.

The Voice in Our Head and the Information It Communicates to Us

Before further discussing the voice in our head, here's an exercise that will give you a practical demonstration of it.

Pause Your Machinery

- I'd like you to put the book down for 45 seconds, remain quiet, and listen to the voice in your head. Then come back to the book and continue with question #2.

_D-JACKSON INT.

ATLANTA, LLC
_o-2635521
ATL AIRP DIVERSE D21/DR3

******* Sale *******

Check: 00323737-1531   POS: 58304420-093
Date: 04/11/2011   Time: 12:56:18

Item	Units		Amount
MY MIND IS NOT ALWAY	1	7%	16.95
SUBTOTAL:	1		16.95
***** TAX 7 %			1.19
TOTAL:			18.14

Payment method	Amount
MASTER CARD [USD]	18.14

**** *******0363
Authoriz. No.:   336727
Merchant ID: v9702080

Thank you for visiting Areas, and please
come again. Comments? Please contact
us at AreasATL@areasmail.com

- What did the voice say? Did it ask you why you were bothering to do this exercise? Or tell you that what you're reading doesn't really apply to you because you always have control over your mind and that your mind's machinery never has control over you? Did it tell you that you don't have any programming that makes dysfunctional decisions for you? That the word machinery, even as a metaphor, doesn't apply to anything about you because you're a human being? Did it tell you that maybe you shouldn't finish reading this book? That maybe it's a waste of your time?

We often assume that our machinery's internal voice tells us "the truth" because "it's pure me." We experience it as our mind talking to us. If the voice says we're wasting our time, it must be because we are wasting our time. After all, it's our own voice in our head telling us this. It couldn't be anyone else's voice other than our own. But this isn't true. Actually, it's every voice we've ever heard and internalized, starting with what our mother and father told us. "Milk will make you strong." "Don't waste money." "If you don't watch yourself, people will take advantage of you." "You have to live up to your potential." Or the opposite: "You don't have any ability, so you might as well forget it."

I believe that this voice, our internal dialogue, goes back millions of years to the beginning of our species and that it has evolved over time and been individualized through a personality DNA, in which it is personalized by our own unique experiences. As I see it, this voice, which is constantly trying to protect us, doesn't always tell us the truth, but I don't believe it is lying to us, either. The reason for this apparently contradictory statement has to do with how the voice is programmed by our machinery.

Our machinery has a massive amount of data coming into its "control center" and uses filters to instantly process these bits of information and put them into what the machinery judges to be the right file. Because of the way the filters work, the machinery often hears what it expects to hear and sees what it expects to see. Here's what I mean.

The mind's machinery responds to every new happening and event by creating a new pattern for response or by reinforcing an existing pattern that was established in response to a past event. Our machinery doesn't always know true from false. Remember, we are gods in our own private universe, and the machinery is programmed to preside over that universe. It is constantly videotaping everything it comes in contact with and storing those videos in its files to accomplish its mission.

The problem is that it sometimes misfiles the videos. For example, a friend says, "You really enjoy your food!" Where does the mind file that? Under "I'm a gourmet" or under "I'm eating too much," "I've just been insulted," or "I'm fat"? Whatever our friend may have meant, it's our interpretation that registers and that determines where it's filed and how we will react to that comment—all based on experiences and interpretations we've stored from the past.

It's the same when, going back to an earlier example, we notice someone giving us a "strange look," and our machinery starts questioning what the look means. Do we file it under, "She likes me," "She hates me," or "Is my fly open?" Whatever file we put it into may be responsible for a long series of events that can help us or hurt us and may continue for this entire lifetime unless we interrupt it. The difficulty is that we are frequently interpreting our experiences based on assumptions and incorrect or incomplete information.

This is why I say that our mind's machinery is not programmed to always tell us the truth; it is programmed to do what it perceives as good for our survival. Ultimately, our machinery is programmed for its own survival, for its continued control over us to do what it thinks is best for us, based on earlier programming. Like HAL, our machinery is set up to get its mission accomplished and it doesn't want interference.

As we've seen, all input is filtered or colored by our machinery.

Because input is filed based on past experience or events, some of it is tainted by past associations that don't apply and that keep us in the past. Wondrous, remarkable things can only happen in the present; they won't come into this tainted, filtered world.

Let's look more closely at how the filter works and how information is interpreted and filed. In constantly judging everything, especially things it perceives as possible survival issues, our machinery attributes meaning to everything, whether it is meaningful or not. Survival issues can be obvious and objectively assessed as issues of survival, as in the case of our walking through a burning building where there really is a mortal threat. Or they can be obscure and perhaps imagined, as in the case of someone giving us what we consider a "strange look" that may, in fact, be benign or even positive but that our machinery, because of past experiences that it associates with the look, interprets as being a threat.

These aren't the only kinds of meaning the machinery can add to the happenings and events we encounter. As the machinery does its constant evaluations, it can be highly critical and filled with cynicism. As it files everything into existing files, if things repeatedly don't go our way, the machinery can interpret the repetition of frustrated expectations and desires into an attitude of cynicism and resignation that becomes part of our programming, and we can start to believe that in the future things will always be the same—bleak. Resignation and cynicism kill all potential for being alive in the moment. Aliveness and joy can't live in an environment that denies their existence.

Like HAL, our machinery is programmed to get its mission accomplished at all costs. Thus it is threatened by any information that can potentially lessen its control. It creates defenses against any input that would disempower it, input that would make us aware that our machinery exists and uncover how it is programmed. These defenses keep us resistant to information that can weaken their hold over us and lead us to self-transformation.

That's why the voice in your head may have said you're wasting your time reading this book. Your machinery isn't set up for you to learn anything that would interrupt it; it is set up to keep doing what it is doing. It's because our machinery is programmed to retain its control that it tends to keep us frozen in place, seeing the world the same way we've always seen it, feeling the same feelings we've always felt. If we've generally been unhappy, as long as we allow our machinery to run us we will continue being generally unhappy.

When we consciously interrupt the machinery and are in the present, the voice in our head may still be there, but it is observational and discerning rather than critical and judgmental and its response is therefore conscious and healthy rather than unconsciously determined, disruptive, and destructive.

By becoming aware of how our particular programming works—identifying the issues that are likely to activate our machinery and cause it to create incorrect interpretations and judgments—we learn to tell the difference between the voice that is prompting an appropriate response and the voice that is biased and likely to lead us to self-destructive behavior.

The next section deals with becoming aware of the specific factors that created our machinery's programming—our unique inner world, how we think and feel, and the situations in which we are likely to become unconscious and to act self-destructively.

PART II

WHAT HAPPENS IN OUR INNER WORLD: HOW WHAT WE DON'T KNOW *CAN* HURT US

CHAPTER SIX
A CLOSE LOOK AT HOW OUR INNER WORLDS WORK

I really started learning how my programming created my behavior when I began therapy 35 years ago. I was 30 and my professional life was great, I was making a lot of money and already had a wonderful house and the trappings of material success. My personal life, however, wasn't so rosy! I was experiencing constant frustration and stress.

I was quick and decisive when it came to business, but the opposite when it came to my closest relationships. I put up with situations that felt almost intolerable and postponed making decisions that would require me to act. The frustrations kept mounting. I was unhappy in my marriage and couldn't bring myself to deal with it. How could I be so clear and productive in business and so stuck in my marriage?

About this time, my mother had a personal crisis and started therapy. I saw how within a few weeks she got back on track, so I called the same therapist, hoping I could get quick comfort and some resolution. I wanted to learn why I was so indecisive in my closest personal relationship and how to fix it.

Talking about my problems in therapy was very satisfying. The therapist, Dr. Haas, listened to me talk about the pain I was feeling without being judgmental and helped me put the issues into focus. No one had ever done that for me in my entire life.

I eased into months of talk therapy, which started with the intention of dealing with my macro issues—life-shaping crises, like what to do about my marriage—and quickly morphed into discussion and problem solving on a never-ending series of "pebble-in-the-shoe problems"—minor, annoying conflicts in my relationships that could nevertheless paralyze me in the same way a pebble caught in one's shoe can make it impossible to walk.

Almost every "pebble" turned out to result from an old core issue that I had been largely unaware of and that had been with me since childhood. In other words, the issues that were causing me to experience the problem in the present were part of my unconscious patterned behavior—my mind's machinery and its programming! Everything was based in the past!

Each question Dr. Haas posed to me seemed to probe more deeply into my inner world and to shed more light on how it was determining my experience of life. Until this point I hadn't realized that not only were my inner-world issues hidden from others, I had hidden them from myself. Becoming more aware of what caused me to act and react as I did was like waking up from sleepwalking. I began to see that my behavior had patterns and that these patterns were related to the coping strategies I had unconsciously invented over the years to deal with—actually to avoid—my feelings.

Gradually I learned that these same coping strategies often made problems linger and added frustration to my relationships. I learned that while I was always saying I wanted closeness and satisfaction in my relationships, my actions robbed me of the closeness and satisfaction I craved. As I became aware of my machinery by seeing my core issues and learning how they were controlling me, I began to see that I could start making conscious choices instead of reacting automatically and unconsciously, and that by doing this I could create movement in my life instead of staying stuck!

Our inner worlds are all different, but the way they are formed is very similar. We're born with what I think of as pre-bundled automatic reflexes, such as crying when we are stuck by a diaper pin, but for the most part our infant mind is a blank slate. We start filling in this blank slate very quickly. Grandmother tickles us and kisses us and the cat takes our tiny toys and we automatically write programming about both experiences, which contains opinions that stay with us forever even though we may continue to modify them.

The opinions in our programming result from our interpretations of events, which were automatically added to each experience. Through these interpretations we invent and create our inner universe. We distinguish or recognize the difference between the hard, ungiving feel of the slats in our baby crib when our head accidentally hits them versus the feel of our mother's soft skin as she gently picks us up and soothingly breastfeeds us, and we add these experiences and interpretations to our universe. We do the same with the people we see and the objects and circumstances we encounter.

The first time we experience it, each item and experience is new to us, and the instant it is incorporated into our programming we are adding it to our personal and unique universe. We have literally invented or created everything in our mind, only it's done unconsciously so we are unaware that it's our own invention. We forget that we invented it—literally made it up. We forget that we created our own universe.

When the voice in our head coming from our machinery speaks about the past, present, or future, it is doing so by downloading the machinery's files and projecting the machinery's perception of the past, present, or future. And remember, this perception is based on the machinery's interpretation of a past experience of an event, a person, or an object.

I love the story about the three blind men who have never seen an elephant and are asked what the elephant looks like. Each of them approaches the beast from a different place. The first touches its leg and says an elephant looks like a tree trunk. The second touches its side and says an elephant looks like a barn. The third touches its trunk and says it looks like a snake. So each blind man's picture of an elephant and the story he tells about it is different from the other blind men's pictures or stories, due to their individual interpretations, based on their individual and limited experience of the elephant.

Similarly, everything our mind processes becomes its own unique tale in its own unique universe, all made up and based on the particular way that we approached a situation.

When our machinery is running us, our particular approach to every situation depends on our past experiences and interpretations, and our interpretation of that situation is formed just as each of the three blind men formed his picture of the elephant: The blind men approached the elephant from different angles, each feeling only part of it but assuming they were objectively experiencing the whole elephant. In the same way we approach an experience through the limited filter provided by the story we bring to that experience.

Again, the problem is that until we become aware of it, we never realize that it's just a tale we made up, our own projection, perceived through our own filter. We forget that we've made the story up and instead believe it to be true.

I'll show you how this works by using an example from my life. We all have issues, or core stories from childhood—I call them "tapes"—which we believe changed the course of our lives. We tell each other how a death, a divorce, an illness, being too fat, too thin, too rich, or too poor, and a thousand other tales—some of which assume the proportions of personal myths—changed the path of our lives from what they were supposed to be. My core story is about my father's sudden and unexpected death at age 38, when I was just 11, and how it changed my life.

I was awakened in the middle of the night by my father's groaning. I tried to help but my mother told me to go outside and wait for the ambulance. I was in shock. A little later, I saw my father being carried into an ambulance on a stretcher with my mother walking and crying right behind him. A few hours later my mother came back into our tiny house clutching his underwear and screaming hysterically, "He's dead."

My 11-year-old machinery went into warp speed. This was ultimate proof that "there is a terrible problem here." Two days later, the "hook" was set on my core story: The rabbi cut my tie in half at the funeral, marking the new, fatherless phase in my life.

We went home to a house filled with grieving people who treated me like a charity case. I didn't understand, and I was scared. I couldn't find my mother. Minutes later I found her alone in our garage, sobbing and repeating over and over, "I want to die." In a millisecond, my 11-year-old machinery went into survival mode: If she committed suicide, I would be an orphan and up the creek without a paddle.

The involuntary words came out of my mouth, "Don't worry, Mom, I will take care of you!"

Therein is the basis for the core story that ran my life for the next 20 years, until I landed in a therapist's office—a married, lonely, professionally successful, and unhappy young man. It was in that office that I got in touch with the anger and resentment that was keeping me stuck and killing off much of the joy in my closest relationships—all of it rooted in this story. On the bright side, this same story holds the roots of my material success.

Later I'll explain the patterns of behavior that I've carried with me since then, with positive effects in the sphere of professional achievements and negative effects in my personal relationships. But first it's important to look at what the core story illustrates about how we make up our tales about ourselves, others, and the world.

I've come to understand that my mother never asked me to take care of her. Looking at the barebones facts, I see I was a kid who couldn't take care of myself, let alone an older brother and a mother. None of the tale I told myself about the events was real; it was just what my machinery mistakenly believed—my interpretation—but, nonetheless, I acted out my part as the one who had to take responsibility and I got better and better at it over the next 20 years. That interpretation would still be determining my behavior today if I hadn't become aware of it and learned that it was just my machinery's tale about what occurred, and that if I kept letting my machinery run me, the joke was on me!

The voice in our head is making meaning out of everything all the time. That is the nature of humans. Whether an incident is big or small, our machinery automatically injects meaning into everything—meaning that we perceive as the truth. The sight of my hysterical mother crying in the garage was so powerful that there was no way I could not tell myself a story (an interpretation) about what I was seeing and then automatically inject that story into my memory of the event.

The mind's machinery then uses this information—its interpretations—as it automatically draws its conclusions about what will be best for our survival. These conclusions determine our behavior. The more traumatic the incident, the more important these strategies for survival are, and the more deeply embedded in our machinery this programming becomes. The more deeply embedded these strategies for survival are, the more likely it is that they will continue controlling our behavior until we become aware of them and learn to stop our machinery from using them in situations in which they are disruptive.

Our Machinery's Relationship to Pain

Besides our strategies for survival being embedded in our programming, every emotional pain we've ever experienced is stored there and has an effect on us, whether we are conscious of it or not. I think of this gathered pain as a giant octopus that lies just beneath our emotional surface. It has tentacles that reach into the physical body as well as a tentacle that reaches directly into the body's mission control center and overrides our normal functioning without our even realizing it.

The mere fear of emotional pain is enough to engage this octopus's tentacles. Every sigh, deep breath, or tightening in the esophagus is a clue that the octopus has taken over. This octopus of pain is also at the heart of most of our feelings of fear, upset, depression, anxiousness, and stress. The greater the fear or the pain, the tighter the tentacles grip us.

The fact that this pain affects our physical bodies is the reason that therapists often point to the physical signs—like holding our breath—that tell us we are experiencing anxiety. But again, the tangible reality of the emotional pain we carry around with us doesn't mean that we're aware of it. Here's what I mean.

In that first session with the therapist, I was asked what my childhood was like. I didn't think for a second, I just responded, "A regular boy's childhood." When I said this, I meant that my childhood was no different from the popular old television series *Father Knows Best* and *Leave It to Beaver*, even though these shows were comedies in which the fathers were very much alive and everything was "perfect."

Why did I say this? I needed to think that my father's death was something I had handled as if it were no big deal. I hated the idea of being seen as a victim and pitied; pity was intolerable to me. It was like being shamed or blamed. I thought of myself as too strong to be a victim. This is one of the things I told myself, and it was part of what I tried to portray to other people. But that didn't mean I was not in pain, even though I didn't always know I was in pain or that sometimes the pain manifested itself in physical ways. I certainly didn't know what was causing it. And I hadn't a clue that the pain I was not aware of was running me. I was in complete denial.

Denial is one of our strongest defenses to ward off pain as well as to block off other feelings that we don't want to have, feelings that our mind judges to be dangerous. My machinery saw my true feelings about the loss of my father as dangerous to my survival, so I unconsciously cut those feelings out, having no idea that it was at the cost of closeness in my deepest relationships for the next 20 years.

When we are in denial about our pain, it always affects our relationships. And our machinery can be in denial about its deepest wounds, even though they become the core of our programming!

It's important to realize that even when we learn how our machinery works and how to interrupt it, the machinery will never go away. We will always be struggling with it. If a person is still on this planet, he or she has machinery, even though the machinery might not always be activated.

When, after five years, I "graduated" from my first course of therapy, I asked the doctor if he had any words of wisdom for me. He said, "You've shed much of your armor but you didn't let it go. You put a string around it and are still dragging it around, so you may keep tripping over it." These defense mechanisms that were meant to keep me from being hurt instead had the effect of keeping me in my own emotional prison. They had cut me off from my feelings and had made it all but impossible for me to experience aliveness and joy.

My therapist was warning me that despite the insight I had gained, I was still carrying these defense mechanisms around with me and was likely to trip over them. In other words, I'd become aware of my programming and learned to interrupt my machinery some of the time, but I needed to know that I would still be struggling with it.

Whether or not we are aware of it, all of us have had childhood traumas that our mind interpreted in specific ways that may still determine our behavior to this day. Gaining insight into our individual core story (or stories) is a good start, but in order to move into the present we need to do more.

Our Machinery's Automatic Setting:
What It Does—and Doesn't Do—for Us

As we've seen, our machinery has automatic responses, like the ones we use when driving a car. If we're driving and something pops up in front of us and we see it, we swerve in order to avoid a collision. We don't debate whether we should swerve or not swerve, we don't even think about it; it's an automatic reaction from our programming. We immediately swerve and after we're safe, we may think about what just happened and its potential consequences. Most of the machinery's actions are done in the same way. For each of us, our machinery has its own unique automatic pilot on instant alert.

Going back to an earlier example, when I perceive that I've been insulted, my automatic response is generally to react instantly, often to my detriment. It's similar to the automatic knee jerk we experience when the doctor taps our kneecap during a physical.

I've become aware of my machinery's automatic settings that are used to avoid pain and upsets in my relationships. This programming echoes my childhood issues surrounding loss and abandonment. These automatic settings are based on my fear of getting hurt, and their mission is to help me avoid getting hurt rather than to support my experiencing what is actually happening in the moment.

The net result is that while I long for closeness, my machinery often pushes the opportunity for the closeness away. When my machinery is running me, I make myself emotionally unavailable—and I have no clue that I'm doing it. Even when I take the chance and get close, my machinery persists in testing that closeness, which is another way of pushing people away.

Remember, our automatic settings are based in the past and are always self-defeating in terms of our ability to be in the present.

My friend Louie explains that the mission of his machinery's automatic setting is "to keep the peace and make sure that I'm not a burden." Louie had an absentee father, a neglected mother, and two sisters, and there was a lot of chaos in his home. Louie describes his family dynamic as "unbalanced."

He told me, "I instinctively learned to minimize my own needs in order to keep the peace and put others first. It may have been false, but it gave me a sense of security and control. Now, as an adult, I've learned that holding on to these old patterns and denying my needs keeps me in a state of mere survival as opposed to thriving. At 40, I consciously struggle with this old behavior. I know that the only way to do this is to transform myself by making conscious choices not to behave in self-destructive old ways. This is the key to my staying out of the prison of my own mind."

Most of us have experienced situations in which we felt trapped. These are the emotional prisons we have placed ourselves into, and either we hold the key and don't use it or we willingly hand the key over to others and let them be our jailers. In such situations, we lose all of our power, either to the people whom we've made our jailers or because we don't acknowledge that we are our own jailers.

If left operating on its own, our machinery will keep us in our prison cell. There are three ways to free ourselves. We can

1. Remove ourselves from the situation.

2. Change the situation.

3. Accept the situation totally.

Why would we stay in a prison cell instead of making one of these choices? Why do we allow our machinery to keep us stuck? One reason we might do this is that our machinery is used to the familiar pain of that cell and it is afraid of what will happen if we break out and experience unfamiliar pain that the machinery believes could be greater than the pain we currently have. This fear of change stops us from being fully alive and results from our machinery's constant and often mistaken programming for survival based on our past.

In the next chapter, we're going to look at how our programming can take over whole areas of our behavior without our being aware of it and what we can do about it.

CHAPTER SEVEN

C. G. JUNG'S CONCEPT ON COMPLEXES: A PSYCHOLOGICAL PERSPECTIVE ON MACHINERY AND PROGRAMMING

Pioneer psychoanalyst Carl G. Jung shines a light on how our programming works from his point of view on human psychology in his discussion of complexes. I've found this very helpful and am sharing it with you as another piece of the puzzle to understand ourselves and overcome our machinery's disruptive programming.

The Jungian therapist Dr. Leana Melat explains that Jung defines complexes as "complete patterns of behavior that operate on their own and live in our unconscious mind."[1] In other words, complexes are specific responses and actions that are part of our machinery's programming and of which we are often unaware.

Because complexes operate on their own—as long as we are not aware of the ways that they cause us to feel and behave—they have the power to possess us. Indeed, when the term complex became popular, Jung wrote that everyone knows nowadays that people have complexes, "what is not so well known…is that complexes can have us."[2] In other words, like the rest of our programming, when complexes are activated, unless we interrupt them, they run us!

According to Jung, part of individuation—the process each of us goes through to become a separate, whole individual—is becoming aware of our complexes and learning to stop them from taking us over. As Dr. Melat expresses it, "Our complexes are the dung heap and our gold is hidden in them."[3] "As people committed to being conscious, our job is to shovel the dung away and expose the gold—our capacity to just be."[4]

Jung describes a complex as a group of ideas or images—ways of seeing the world and reacting to it—that are often incompatible with the conscious mind and the way we consciously think of ourselves. He calls complexes "splinter psyches"[5] or mini-personalities in the psyche, the term Jung uses for all our mental processes, conscious and unconscious.[6] He explains that the origin of complexes is frequently a trauma, which splits off a bit of the psyche, relegating it to the unconscious because the conscious mind finds our authentic emotional response to the trauma—hurt and anger, for example—unacceptable. The complex or mini-personality is born from this split and then begins operating automatically as long as we remain unaware of it.

Thus, like all our programming, we do not consciously ask our complexes to be born, but as adults we must take responsibility for becoming aware of them, reducing them, and controlling them.

As you'll see, once we learn about complexes, they can become easy to recognize because they have such an enormous emotional charge. (Remember, when our machinery is activated, it takes over our nervous system and produces a frenzy of feelings such as anxiety, stress, fear, and internal conflict or going unconscious and wanting to fall asleep.)

Dr. Melat says that we develop complexes over our lifetime, starting in infancy, from repeated emotional stress, and that they cluster around specific archetypes. From a Jungian perspective, archetypes, she explains, are "the patterns of thought and behavior which are common to humanity through all time."[7] We can look at the Woolly Mammoth Age's pre-bundled programming as containing many of our human archetypes.

As Jung saw it, two of the most prominent archetypes are the Mother archetype and the Father archetype. We can think of it this way: All of us are born with the need for nurturing and support by a mother and a father, and we come into this world with certain unconscious, universal images about what "mother" and "father" should be. Jung believed that we inherit these images in our very brain structure from what he called the "collective unconscious" that is inborn because it is part of every human psyche, passed on from generation to generation.

An example of how a mother complex develops is that all negative or stressful events around mother issues (nurturance, love, acceptance by others, self-acceptance) cluster together. You could have a mother complex if, for example, starting in your infancy your mother ignored some of your basic needs. This could arise from various circumstances, such as your mother being overworked or distracted or from her not having had some of her basic needs met during her own childhood and therefore not knowing how to recognize and meet yours.

Because a child's dependency on his or her mother is so strong, you can develop a mother complex and still feel close to your mother since, until you become conscious of your programming, you may be unaware that some of your important needs have not been met. You may even tend to be drawn to or feel close to anyone who produces feelings in you like the feelings your mother produced. When this happens, the person may actually be neglecting your needs just the way your mother did. We may think that's what love is.

A complex that forms around nurturing issues can also block your ability to recognize and take care of the needs of others because your mother never modeled empathy. The complex can block your ability to take care of your own true needs, too, even if you think you are taking care of them, because you are still unconscious of what your true needs are.

A complex grows larger with each negative event in our lives, robbing the psyche of the amount of energy available to the consciousness. At some point, the complex has more energy than the consciousness, and that's when it can take us over automatically and "possess us." When complexes possess us, they create the feeling of being trapped in an emotional prison, which we discussed earlier.

Another example of a mother complex can occur if a young boy experiences his mother as continually making arbitrary or unfair rules. He can then develop a mother complex that in adulthood makes him respond to strong women with discomfort, suspicion, and defensiveness, and he might avoid them.

Alternatively, he may seek out a strong woman as a mate and willingly or resentfully be submissive to her, or he may continually rebel against her. Even if he's aware that he experienced his mother as arbitrary or unfair, when the complex is activated, it takes over his perceptions and behavior so, until he has learned about the complex and its power over him, he may be unaware that it has taken over. He's likely to be angry, but he won't necessarily know why.

A young girl who experiences an arbitrary or unfair mother can develop a mother complex that, as she grows up, can make her distrustful of friendships and feel a lack of confidence in herself. The complex can contribute to insecurity in her opinions and decisions and can make her unable to think clearly for herself.

The difference between the mother complex of a boy and of a girl who perceive their mothers in this way arises because a daughter, being the same gender as her mother, experiences her mother as a source of nurturing and as a role model, which undermines her experience of herself as well as of others. A boy, almost from birth, knows that he is "other" than his mother and therefore doesn't have to emulate her—her behavior is separate from himself. Thus, his mother complex is likely to make him attribute these qualities to the opposite sex.

An example of how a father complex develops is that all negative or emotionally stressful events around father issues (providing guidance for how to be in the world and setting boundaries and limits) cluster together. If, for instance, a boy's father is emotionally distant or partially or fully absent, the boy may develop a father complex that makes him feel insignificant in the world and insecure about how to act in it.

Alternatively, the boy may develop a father complex that makes him feel—as I did, after my father's death—that he must make up for the absent father and achieve in the world. A father complex can also make him seek other males—teachers, professional mentors, religious leaders, therapists—to be the father he never had. A father complex can make him seek accolades from the world—as I did—in order to make up for the affirmation that the absent father was never able to give. (As Dr. Melat pointed out to me, my mother and father complexes made me a "do-er.")

A girl with a distant or absent father can develop a father complex that makes her struggle with the issue of financial accomplishment and economic success. The complex might also make her attracted to men as potential partners who cannot be fully present for her—in keeping with her experience of her distant or absent father. The unavailable man she seeks may be a workaholic, or he may stay out late at night with his male friends or be promiscuous with other women. Essentially, her father complex has eerily populated her outer world and become alive in her surroundings. What she's always hoping for is that she can get the man she's pursuing to make the change her father couldn't.

The examples we've looked at describe the way particular individuals might respond to how they have been parented and the ways that the resulting mother and father complexes affect them. The same parenting circumstances will impact another individual differently, depending on the particular nature of the child—for example, if he or she is introverted or extroverted—and how sensitive the child is to others and their needs. We are all born with different characteristics that make us unique, just as our fingerprints are unique.

Although the specific details of our complexes vary for each of us, Jung says that, essentially, complexes are unavoidable. If our parents have been clearly deficient in parenting us or if they have emotionally or physically harmed us, it's obvious that we will have developed complexes. But even if we are parented with fairly good parenting, Jung emphasizes that in the first five years of our lives we inevitably learn to repress parts of our natural selves that may be very healthy but that don't meet our parents' needs or expectations. We adapt to our parents' requirements in order to survive and in doing so we automatically develop complexes that become part of our programming.

Another way of putting this is that no mother and father can meet all of their children's needs, and therefore all of us have mother and father complexes that vary in their type and degree of intensity, depending on the parenting we've had and our own individual nature.

Regardless of a complex's specific characteristics, all complexes are disruptive in that they make us behave in ways that are unconscious and often dysfunctional and that make it impossible for us to be in the present. Jung says that no matter how much work we do on ourselves we will never be completely rid of our complexes, and the basic structure of complexes will leave their remnants in our personalities. But we can shrink them down to a manageable size—meaning that we can learn to recognize that a complex is being activated and catch ourselves before it completely takes us over. We can interrupt it!

This is what Dr. Haas meant when he told me that even though I had shed some of the armor of my defenses, I was still carrying around the armor tied to my foot and I had to be careful not to trip over it. Although we may have periods when we experience being complex free, we may find them starting to be activated again, and that's when we have to do our work!

According to Dr. Melat, this is how we can think about the work of interrupting our complexes: Complexes are essentially one sided because they contain only one attitude and prompt one kind of behavior. To combat a complex, we have to learn to act from its opposite side, and this will immediately break the complex and allow us to change our behavior.

Let's go back to the example of a man with a mother complex that makes him suspicious of strong women. If a man with this type of mother complex meets a strong woman and finds himself distancing himself from her before he's even allowed himself the chance of responding to who she truly is, then to combat the complex he can take a deep breath and slow down.

Once he has slowed down, he can look at his pre-programmed responses, recognize that they are coming from his complex, and consciously shift his attitude to listening to her and really hear her with an open mind. This will completely change his behavior because the complex doesn't have its hold over him. (See chapter 15 for more details about how to do this.)

Remember, according to Jung, the work of becoming separate, whole individuals requires that we become aware of our complexes. Jung emphasizes that "a complex becomes pathological [diseased] only when we think we have not got it."[8] It's only as long as you are not conscious of how it makes you feel and behave that a complex has the power to possess you.

When we're in a complex, we lose our ability to have sound judgment and to respond with appropriate emotions to what is happening in the present. If we don't know about the complex, we will react according to what the complex dictates and be driven by it.

As Jung describes it, each complex steals a certain amount of our psychic energy. Jung associates this psychic energy with our libido, that part of our psyche with energy from what he calls the "natural urge of life," including the sex drive and, as he defines it, the spiritual drive.[9]

Each of us has only a limited amount of libido, and if a complex is using too much of this psychic energy, it causes us to feel awful. Jung says that a libido has a mind of its own. When we are run by our complexes and our life force is therefore depleted, we may become depressed. A depressed person, Jung observes, feels lost, tired, and deeply defeated.

Jung observes that when the libido seems to disappear as it does in depression, it must appear in another form, which then becomes a symptom of an unresolved complex. Thus depression or another symptom of libido depletion, such as anxiety, fear, internal conflict, or guilt, is a sign of a complex's hold over us and it signals that the complex is determining our experience of the world. According to Jung, when we experience a symptom of a complex, it is actually a gift because it tells us we have work to do.

Dr. Melat emphasizes that dismantling the complex, brick by brick, requires the daily hard work of "observing ourselves and how we react to stimuli and of transforming our perceptions, beliefs, attitudes, and responses or behavior."[10] When we can successfully transform the complex's perceptions, beliefs, and attitudes, we feel freer.

This, of course, is what we're working toward in this book. The process of dismantling our complexes is a vital part of learning to be conscious of our machinery and to interrupt it, of learning how to manage our machinery instead of allowing it to manage us. The next step in this process is to look clearly at our own behavior—not only how we as human beings act in general, but also how we as specific individuals act, why we do what we do, and when and why it doesn't always serve us.

CHAPTER EIGHT

HOW WE PRESENT OURSELVES TO THE WORLD AND WHAT IT COSTS US

We've seen how the machinery constantly monitors and records the input of our five senses and uses it to accomplish its master goal of doing what it judges to be necessary to help us survive. We've also seen how it does not always file accurately, without bias, the information it takes in. It's never "just the facts." The machinery often filters and interprets the information, seeing what it expected to see and hearing what it expected to hear. We've seen how these tainted observations become the stories that create our machinery's programming and that influence or determine our behavior.

Herein lies the source of most of our emotional problems and pain because, as we've seen, the stories are our view of what happened, not necessarily what really happened. The machinery frequently twists our perceptions in ways that create painful experiences where these perceptions might not really apply. Very often this goes back to our machinery's tendency to mistakenly label issues as issues of survival.

I know the word survival sounds melodramatic when applied to our daily lives; we don't generally think that our everyday interactions with people can get us killed. But it's the woolly mammoth factor again: the fear of being ostracized—cut off from the tribe—reaches back to our 2.5-million-year-old programming, which takes over and makes our mind believe that our survival is at stake even when it's not. It's why being lonely in our modern psyches can feel like we're going to die; we would have died if we were on our own, separated from our tribe, in the woolly mammoth days. Any issue that feels like a survival issue activates our machinery. It can even be intensely activated by someone not treating us as warmly as we would like.

Our machinery's primary way of dealing with its fear of being thrown out of the tribe is to find ways to be wanted and needed by others. Thus, we look for ways to be considered valuable or admired. Whether we know it or not, most of us are constantly seeking to be validated by the tribe. We may define validation as standing out and being superior or as simply being acceptable or even not being noticed. However we define it, we are seeking approval or validation so that we will not be singled out for the rejection we consciously or unconsciously fear.

The important points to recognize in terms of our behavior are that we are seeking to be accepted, that our machinery has a never-ending need for approval or validation, and that it has many strategies, often unconscious, for achieving it.

Our Persona and How It Can Keep Us Trapped

Each of us has our own distinct way of conducting ourselves with others. We are a bucket filled with characteristics such as our name, height, weight, family background, race, religion, job, looks, and hundreds of other qualities, including personality traits and attitudes. The sum of these characteristics makes up how we present ourselves to the world.

A large part of what we and others think of as us as individuals is the way we act and react. We can be risk-takers or non risk-takers, leaders or followers, trusting or skeptical, or take on any number of other patterns of behavior that become how we present ourselves and how the rest of the world perceives us. In other words, the personality, the character that you play—your persona—becomes what people think of as you. Once formed, the strong patterns of behavior that become your persona are hard to break out of. By becoming conscious of the specific ways that we present ourselves to the world, we can recognize how the character—or more accurately, the characters—we play in our daily lives keep us from being in the now.

The way I think of it, we are like certain character actors who appear in films and TV shows who, regardless of the particular script, always seem to be the same: the smart friend, the sexy bimbo, the eccentric uncle, the cantankerous guy, the creep, the jokester, the psycho, the understanding grandfather or grandmother. They are typecast over and over again.

Similarly, our machinery and its programming, including our complexes, keep us stuck playing the same roles over and over. We trap ourselves into attitudes and points of view that the machinery uses both to represent and to justify our character. As long as we remain on automatic pilot, we're always playing one of these characters. When we are doing this, we are eliminating the possibilities of freeing ourselves from old patterns and being in the now. If we are rigid and continue acting the same ways we've always behaved, we leave little room for new possibilities and we are stuck in this mold that becomes our permanent personality and behavior.

Pause Your Machinery

- Has a friend or family member ever told you that you (your personality, not your looks) remind him or her of a certain character in a movie, TV show, or book? If so, write the name or a description of the character.

- Do you see a resemblance between yourself and this character?

- Describe what it is about the way you act or present yourself that you think reminds your friend or family member of this character.

- Is there a social role, such as caretaker, leader, or peacemaker that others often identify you as filling or that you identify with and feel you should fill?

- Do you see yourself as playing this role?

- Now think of scenarios where you could more or less predict how your character or someone who exemplifies your social role would react. Describe the scenario and, in one or two sentences, tell what your character would do. For example, what would the character do if he or she tripped in front of a roomful of people? How would he or she discipline a toddler who dropped a new digital camera in the toilet? How would he or she react if criticized by a boss? How would he or she react walking in on colleagues or family members fighting with each other?

Remember, unless we learn to interrupt our machinery, no matter how spontaneous we may think we are, our way of interacting with other people is programmed on an unconscious level and we are responding with programming created in the past. By doing this, we are keeping the past alive and making it our future.

The Evolution of Our Persona

I believe that although, for each of us, our persona—how we present ourselves to the world—is unique and filled with individual quirks, the process by which all personae evolve follows a general pattern:

1. When we are born, we are relatively free of programming, as close as we get to the Garden of Eden days before the serpent.

2. Something happens (a trauma) and our machinery interprets it as a threat to our survival, drawing the conclusion that "There's a terrible problem here" and "I'm not safe."

3. The old woolly mammoth DNA from prehistoric days kicks in, the machinery jumps into our driver's seat and has us do something to mitigate the problem and assure our place in the tribe (which could be just Mom and Dad). We develop complexes and learn adapting skills—being cute, crying, or countless additional sophisticated maneuvers—which, over time, by trial and error, morph us into "people pleasers," "entertainers," "bullies," "sex machines," and all the other personae or roles that people develop.

4. We get used to the belief that "There's a terrible problem here" as well as other beliefs such as "I'm not lovable," "I'm a loser," "I'm superior," and other self-evaluation labels, and these be-

liefs become incorporated into our machinery's programming about who we are. These beliefs become the mold that we are stuck inside of, our set way of presenting ourselves.

5. All of this is repeated and repeated over the course of our lives as our programming keeps us scheming to stay safe and we have no idea what is actually going on. The parts we play as a result collectively become our persona, and we remain unconscious that it's all in our machinery!

Unless we change this dynamic, the die is cast, and we will keep creating a future that will be exactly like our past.

<hr />

Why Our Machinery Likes to Keep Us Stuck— and the Cost of Being Stuck

Rigidly adhering to the same old ways of presenting ourselves to the world, with the repetitive, unconscious actions they consist of, has some consequences that our machinery misguidedly judges to be rewards. These "rewards" are all some form of justifying our behavior and feelings while finding ways to blame other people. The reason the machinery perceives these as rewards is that it uses justifying our behavior and feelings and blaming others as strategies to help achieve its goal of our being accepted by the tribe.

But the cost of being stuck in our set way of presenting ourselves is huge. Being stuck in our character, our persona, costs us freedom of expression, satisfaction, fulfillment, vitality, and well-being. It makes it impossible to truly connect with others, and therefore it makes it impossible to get the love we crave. Having a set way of presenting ourselves keeps us unconscious. It keeps us stuck in our past and re-creates that past into our future, killing off all potential for our experiencing something new and different. How can we experience anything new and different if we are stuck in our old ways? The following truths help to keep me mindful of remaining aware of why it's vital to interrupt my machinery so that I don't have to pay the costs of remaining in a set way of being:

- Joy comes from being in the now, and we are never in the now when our machinery is in the driver's seat.

- The potential for new experiences can only exist when we are free of our machinery and are being true to ourselves—just being. This uncharted territory is the land where the remarkable and the wondrous are possible.

- What we often think of as our feelings come from this set way of being—the self with a small "s"—and come from our machinery's responding to being activated. Often we feel that these feelings control us. The Self with a capital "S" is not a set way of being under the control of our machinery; it is just being. When we are just being, we experience the full range of our feelings and we're not controlled by them.

To help you become aware of and break free from the set way of being your mind's machinery has created for you, here's a closer look at how we evolve the characters that become how we present ourselves to the world and the kinds of characters we may play.

An Assortment of Characters for an Assortment of Situations

Over time, our machinery creates the characters we play as part of its coping strategies for dealing with perceived problems. Though there may be one major character we play much of the time, all of us actually have an assortment of characters in our repertoire. The machinery invented them to elicit different responses from others in different situations. This is why earlier I referred to the characters we play in our daily lives. In other words, although I've talked about each of us having a persona—a set way of presenting ourselves to the world—in reality, this persona is made up of different sub-personae—different sub-personalities and characters— that we unconsciously slip into for different circumstances.

One of my old characters, for example, is "Poor Me—the boy whose father died when he was 11 and who made a success of himself but who still needs your help emotionally, and you're bad if you don't help him." This character often gets activated when my programming tells me I'm being shamed or blamed. The perception that I'm being shamed or blamed has the subtext "I'm bad!" which takes me right back to the woolly mammoth days and the fear of being thrown out of the tribe. I'm back to "There is a terrible problem here" and "I'm not safe." And, by hook or by crook, I've got to change that situation.

The "hook or crook" are my coping strategies, which generally can be looking for sympathy with my "Poor Me" character or going on the attack or becoming defensive or charming—anything to get the attention off being "bad" and to establish that I shouldn't be shamed or blamed. The "Poor Me" character is part of my set way of being and so are the coping strategies.

In learning to let go of our set ways of presenting ourselves to the world, it's important to remember that how we present ourselves to the world isn't really us; it isn't our being. It is simply a construct of our machinery and its fear. Our way of presenting ourselves to the world is an automatic response of our machinery that costs us aliveness and joy. Whenever we are into our set way of presenting ourselves, we are not in the now, and because of this, when we are into our set way of presenting ourselves, we are never being authentic, we are never fully present for ourselves or for others.

With the goal of helping you to recognize your own characters, I'm going to share with you some of the other characters in my persona. I'll also share with you some characters of other people with whom I have worked. My purpose is to show you how these characters arose from our machinery's interpretation of childhood events. It took me years to be clear about these characters. I'm embarrassed to admit that I still slip back into mine when I get activated and don't make the effort to be conscious.

When we were children, our machinery often interpreted the world as scary. It had war, earthquakes, fires, and, for me personally, many cuts and bruises. Our machinery believed it had to be on guard all the time: "Don't rest! Sharpen your wits! Stay ahead of everyone! That's the way to be safe." Out of this thinking came the following characters.

"YOU CAN'T STOP ME!"

"You Can't Stop Me!" is my character that says I must do what I think is right no matter how it affects others. It's a way of being a leader—tribes need leaders.

At five years old, my prized possession was a new portable radio, which was about the size of a toaster, with a leather case and a shoulder strap. While in the car on the highway, on a family outing, I noticed that the radio's shoulder strap was caught in the car door. I asked my dad to stop the car, but he wouldn't. "You Can't Stop Me!" was born, and I opened the car door to retrieve the strap anyway. It was one of those old cars with what were later called "suicide doors," and I was flung out into the middle of the busy highway. A huge drama ensued. I should have been killed, but I survived and got my way. I was almost invincible!

As an adult when I go into this character, everybody is my dad and none of them can stop me.

"MR. CLEANHANDS"

"Mr. Cleanhands" is designed to tell the world that "I'm the good guy. I didn't do anything wrong." Our machinery hates to take responsibility for making problems. More woolly mammoth logic: If we make problems, we get thrown out of the tribe.

For me, my "Mr. Cleanhands" character arose from a childhood shoving match that ended with the other kid tripping and receiving a cut on his head. My eight-year-old machinery thought I would be put in jail, and I hid in my backyard waiting for the police. After that, I had to be "Mr. Cleanhands" so the tribe would never throw me out.

"THE DESIGNATED HITTER"

As "The Designated Hitter," we become the guy the baseball coach puts in the batting lineup to rescue the game. We feel compelled to be a "stand-up" guy or gal who can be counted on to hit a home run. If we strike out by not solving a problem (translation: If we find out we were wrong), our inner world becomes unglued. Being "right" seems to hold everything together.

At the heart of "The Designated Hitter" character is the fear that if we don't do something ourselves, it may not get done and we won't be safe. We become the responsible one who takes care of others when we think they won't do a proper job for themselves. How can a tribe not love this kind of person? The problem is that we do it whether it's appropriate or not. It's exactly what I did at 11 years old when I said I'd take care of my widowed mother.

"THE STAR"

"The Star" is the character we might use in social situations to get adulation and fend off possible rejection. One of my friends used to dance for his parents and their friends when he was little. He loved the applause. The tribe is always going to love the "little entertainer," so he has his repertoire of stories and jokes and ways of being outrageous and even shocking. It is a character that shows how clever and un-self-conscious we are. This character is a response to "There's a terrible problem here" and "I don't fit in." "The Star" character is charming in order to keep our spot and not be rejected.

"POOR ME—THE BOY WHOSE FATHER DIED "

The character I mentioned earlier, "Poor Me—the boy whose father died when I was 11, who needs your help, and you're bad if you don't help me" is a way of asking for a "get-out-of-jail-free card" because you should feel sorry for me.

We use this character when we ask for a free pass when we hurt the feelings of the people closest to us. It tells them that we can't help it because we never learned the appropriate emotional responses as a child.

Many people also use the "Be Tender, I'm Damaged" character—a variation of "Poor Me"—when they want other people to forgive their failings without having to change.

"THE LEGEND"

Over the years I've used "The Legend" character as a way to cover up feelings of inadequacy, hoping that by building a larger-than-life image no one could detect my fears of being a fraud. For me "The Legend" character came out of a belief that if I could enhance my life with possessions and accoutrements, I could show others that I was solid and therefore I would feel solid inside.

By creating a legend about ourselves, we are seeking to avoid feeling second rate and empty—variations of "There is a terrible problem here" and "I don't fit in." Yet trophies, like an expensive car and a big house, aren't enough to overcome that sense of emptiness. Ultimately, this clears the way for the realization that our problems are on the inside and not the outside. When we go into "Legend" mode we become like the Wizard of Oz, who needed to project a larger-than-life image to convince the citizens of Oz that he wasn't a fraud.

Pause Your Machinery

Write your responses to the following:

- In addition to the character or social role you identified earlier, can you come up with other characters you frequently play? For example, do you have a character that portrays you as the hero? The victim or martyr? The expert? Give a name to each character in your repertoire and describe each one's traits.

- Identify and describe the situations or circumstances you associate with these characters. For example, when you go to a party is there a certain character you tend to play? How about when you visit your parents? Attend a company meeting? Ask someone, or get asked, out on a date, or spend an evening alone with your mate?

- Identify and describe the kinds of reactions your machinery is seeking to elicit from others when you play these roles. How do you behave in each of these characters to get acknowledgment? Approval? To justify your actions or be right? To blame others?

Why Our Characters May Be Inconsistent

In doing the above exercise you've begun to identify your own repertoire of characters and the situations you slip in and out of with them. As you start to reflect on your various characters, you may notice that they are not consistent with each other.

For example, I've used "The Designated Hitter" character and the "Mr. Cleanhands" character, and while the stand-up guy part of "The Designated Hitter" is consistent with the "I would never intentionally do anything wrong" part of "Mr. Cleanhands," my desire to avoid responsibility when a problem comes up—God knows it can't be my fault!—is at odds with "The Designated Hitter's" approach to being the one who takes control of situations.

Remember, we have different characters, with different ways of behaving, for different situations, so our characters don't have to be consistent with each other. Remember, too, that our characters are what we do to make ourselves feel safe; they are characters we play, not the truth. It's crucial to recognize that our characters are part of our defenses, and our defenses are ways of avoiding what we fear.

The old warning that even though I'd shed many of my defenses, they were still tied to my foot and I had to be careful not to trip on them is true again: We never completely shed our characters, and so we must always strive to be aware of them.

It takes hard-earned self-awareness to recognize our set ways of being and to overcome them and let them go. It took a long time for me to recognize that my core story—the story of my father's death and its consequence and feeling that I had to be tough, completely self-sufficient, responsible for everyone around me, and never "wrong"—was just the story of my past, and that if I didn't like the tale I was telling about it, I could choose a new one that would allow me to commit to being vulnerable, passionate, open, and in the now. When we feel closed off emotionally, it's because the story we are currently telling ourselves supports this. If that's the case, why not choose a new story that allows us the potential to emotionally nourish others and have them emotionally nourish us?

Why do we resist doing this? What is it about our inner world that makes it challenging to put our stories and set ways of presenting ourselves in the past and to leave them there, thereby creating a positive and unlimited future? In the next chapter we'll take a closer look at the way our beliefs influence our actions and our ways of presenting ourselves and why our beliefs keep us stuck until we become conscious of them. It's only after we develop this awareness that we can let go of our old, dysfunctional stories and create new ones that more accurately represent who we authentically are.

CHAPTER NINE

OUR ORGANIZING PRINCIPLES:
THE CONSCIOUS AND UNCONSCIOUS BELIEFS
THAT CAUSE US TO ACT AS WE DO

The patterns of behavior we form in early childhood are generally triggered by our reactions to how we are received by parents, siblings, and others close to us. Take for an example a child who spills her milk and experiences her dad's response of getting furious, versus that same child if Dad responded by saying, "Don't worry, it's easy to clean up" and reassured her of his love for her. Each of the father's possible reactions and the child's reaction to his reaction can start a lifelong pattern of behavior.

In the case of the father's reacting angrily to the spilled milk, depending on the child's self-image and whether her relationship with her father up to that point has been largely positive or negative, she may react by (1) being a little upset and soon getting over it or (2) deciding that she will be super-careful never to "be clumsy" again so that she won't give him a reason to be angry with her, or (3) deciding, consciously or unconsciously, to do other things that will provoke her father's anger so that he will at least pay some kind of attention to her.

As time goes on, these kinds of themes get more sophisticated and the resulting patterns become deeply ingrained. Eventually these patterns, which are rooted in our complexes, turn into the filters that the machinery uses to review every event we encounter. For good or for bad, the way these filters process what happens to us triggers our subsequent responses.

These filters are our mind's beliefs about the world and our particular place in it, and they also determine what we believe we should expect from it. I call these beliefs our Organizing Principles. They are the guidelines that determine our actions and thus become the basis of our manual for what our standard operating procedures should be. When we're on automatic pilot, our Organizing Principles generally set the tone for how we react to each event.

Picture Organizing Principles as lenses through which the machinery scans each new experience in order to choose what it believes to be the correct reaction. Under the right circumstances, any event can be impactful enough to trigger a child's machinery to create an Organizing Principle that will last a lifetime.

Depending on the patterns of behavior that a child has been developing at home with his parents as well as what the child encounters on the playground—the first-time childhood experience of playing in a sandbox and sharing toys, for example—can lead a child to the Organizing Principle "Kids play with me and it's fun" or "Kids steal my toys." The Organizing Principle may become that sharing brings love or that sharing brings loss, and either may have a far-reaching result.

I have a friend who just can't share his food. When we went to the movies as teenagers, if his date took some of his popcorn or a sip of his drink he wouldn't touch it again. I have another friend who lives his life with the Organizing Principle "If I have a dollar, I'll give my friends 50 cents!" It's "I don't share" versus

"Half of whatever I have is yours." Imagine how these opposite Organizing Principles that govern sharing seep into other attitudes about possessions and impact their lives without their necessarily realizing it.

Another example: A classroom teacher asks for volunteers to answer a question. A correct answer may lead to praise, while an incorrect answer may lead to humiliation. The meaning that a child's machinery may infer from the teacher's and class's response can develop into a lifelong pattern of thinking, "I'm smart" or "I'm stupid," and the birth of Organizing Principles such as "Always stand out" or "Never stand out" and "Volunteering is good" or "Volunteering is bad."

Until we become aware of what our Organizing Principles are and make conscious choices about them, the machinery's constant filtering of current experiences utilizing these past-based Organizing Principles determines the course of our lives. This is the reason I believe that most of the time we hear what we expect to hear and see what we expect to see—because our Organizing Principles—our beliefs based on our interpretations of past experiences, inextricably tied to our complexes—predispose us to do so.

To show you how our Organizing Principles work, I'll describe some of the ones I've discovered in myself. They all stem from my machinery's number one goal: survival!

Please note: I'm aware of these Organizing Principles and strive not to be run by them, and still they constantly seep back into my actions. They are like my shadow on a sunny day: My shadow is always connected to me and I generally have no clue that it's there. Despite my having become aware of my Organizing Principles, they are silently waiting in the wings, ready to kidnap my actions as soon as my machinery thinks it smells danger. Then my machinery will stay in control until I become aware of what is happening and make the conscious effort to be in the present.

These are some of the Organizing Principles in my programming:

1. The world isn't safe; don't trust.

2. Painful feelings are dangerous.

3. I must stay in control to be safe.

4. No one will take care of my needs but me.

5. Hang in there. I can make things happen.

6. Avoid rejection and abandonment: Don't risk losing the love attachment bond.

7. Relationships between parents and children take precedence over all other relationships.

8. I'm not qualified to handle painful situations. That takes a real adult, and in my inner world I'm still a vulnerable kid.

9. If they (anyone close to me) loved me, they would never put me in a terrible position.

10. Eventually, loving others will turn out.

11. I'm a good guy and I never hurt anyone unjustly.

All of my Organizing Principles are inextricably tied to my set ways of presenting myself, and many of my characters grew out of them. As an example, my "Mr. Cleanhands" character grew out of my Organizing Principle "I'm a good guy, and I never hurt anyone unjustly." Many of my Organizing Principles are related to the question of whether I can trust other people to meet my needs or whether I need to be solely responsible for meeting them myself. Organizing Principle #9 is related to an old mistaken belief of mine, that people who really love me should take care of me the way I think I deserve to be taken care of without my having to ask, and if they do anything that causes me emotional distress, it means they don't really love me.

Pause Your Machinery

Write your responses to the following:

- List any of the Organizing Principles I've described that resonate as beliefs that you've held.

- If my Organizing Principles don't seem to be the same as yours—that's to be expected! We all have different patterns. As a starting place for identifying your own, take the opposite of a few of my principles. Do these thought patterns ring a bell? For example, if "No one will take care of my needs but me," doesn't ring true for you, is your Organizing Principle "I can't take care of my own needs; I'm completely dependent on other people"? Or if "Hang in there. I can make things happen" doesn't ring true for you, perhaps your Organizing Principle is "There's no point in hanging in there; I can't make anything happen." Look at the opposites of each of my Organizing Principles and see if any fit as Organizing Principles for you.

- Do any other Organizing Principles that have not yet been mentioned occur to you as beliefs by which you have been running your life?

- Can you see an association between the Organizing Principles you've identified as yours and the characters or roles you tend to play, as described in chapter 8? Explain any relationships you see between them.

As I've mentioned, there are always exceptions to the way our programming works. The machinery isn't logical and doesn't always follow its own rules. Just as there are inconsistencies among our different acts, our Organizing Principles are sometimes inconsistent and in conflict with each other. The machinery resolves these contradictions by creating bizarre rationalizations that can justify these opposite positions.

Our Organizing Principles can keep us in self-defeating loops or binds, repeating patterns of behavior that kill new possibilities, yet we don't feel able to do anything about them. In order to live a life worth living, we must understand how we allow them to do this.

Here's what I mean about the way our Organizing Principles can keep us in a self-defeating bind: My Organizing Principle "Eventually, loving others will turn out" came out of my belief that if I hang in there, no matter how painful the situation, over time I will finally get the love and closeness I desire. But—and this is a big BUT—this Organizing Principle is in direct opposition to my other Organizing Principles that say "Don't trust," "No one will take care of my needs but me," and "If they loved me, they wouldn't have put me in this terrible position."

How can it ever "turn out" if what I want to turn out—getting love and closeness from others—is dependent on my loving people I won't trust? How can I expect people to instinctively know what causes me pain and anticipate my needs and desires if I haven't "clued them in"? How can I expect them to take care of my needs anyway when my Organizing Principle says that "No one will take care of my needs but me"?

It's common sense that these conflicting Organizing Principles have put me into the binds that have created so much of my emotional pain. My Organizing Principles have kept me stuck and unfulfilled!

Here's another bind I've put myself into with these mistaken beliefs. Observe how combining these beliefs made it absolutely impossible for me to have the experience of life that consciously I wanted!

- I can't risk losing the love and attachment bond.

- I can't say "No" to people I really love because that might make them leave me.

- If they really loved me they wouldn't ask me for something that I would have to say "No" to. Instead, they would say "No" for me, the way a good parent would take care of his or her child.

- People close to me won't do this for me.
- So I conclude the people I really love don't really love me.

As you can see, our Organizing Principles, energized by our complexes, can keep us in a loop that denies us the potential for fulfillment and keeps us re-experiencing past pain. The machinery doesn't care if its programming is irrational or if ultimately it's dysfunctional. We keep bumping into the same walls over and over again because we are not programmed for what will make us fully alive; we are programmed only for what the machinery judges will work for survival.

For years my mind enforced my contradictory assumptions and rules, believing they would help me avoid and survive pain. I now see that the opposite happened. These Organizing Principles led to the very pain I was trying to avoid. Remember, past-based assumptions and rules keep us stuck—in the past!

My Organizing Principle that "Painful feelings are dangerous and must be gotten rid of quickly" is an outgrowth of past pain. In fact, this pain made me want to get rid of all my feelings because unconsciously they scared me. I had great difficulty with feelings because I dreaded more pain, so I pushed my feelings aside and developed an assortment of ways to get around them. I've done this by avoiding confrontations, "splitting off" my anger and disowning it, "splitting off" my fear and disowning it, detouring around feeling empty, and seeking validation.

Many people I know also have Organizing Principles that make them avoid confrontations, so I want to spend a moment looking at this common pattern of behavior. We may feel relieved (at least temporarily) to have avoided a confrontation or we may feel that avoiding it has left us frustrated, anxious, and/or stressed. But regardless of how we feel, we don't always realize what avoiding a confrontation costs us; we're not always aware that in order to avoid feeling the emotions and facing the issues that we fear the confrontation will raise, we are giving up our power and shirking our responsibility to ourselves and, sometimes, even to others.

Here's an example of how I've avoided confrontations and what it can cost. Let's say I take my child to buy the latest electronic game. The child looks at the assortment and says, "I want that one (the most expensive, top-of-the-line game with every accessory)." I say, "I wasn't planning on spending that much." My child is quickly in tears, saying, "I hate you." I am reduced to an emotional mess, willing to do anything to regain my child's love. I will buy my way out of that situation in a second! All because my machinery is afraid to risk the loss of my child's affection because I've said "No."

In this situation, my Organizing Principle takes over: "I'm not qualified to handle painful situations. That takes a real adult, and in my inner world I'm still a kid." Without even knowing it, my inner world instantly replays old childhood fears of abandonment (Organizing Principle #6: "Don't risk losing the love attachment bond"), and, bingo, my sense of self is knocked out and my inner world is acting in a state of panic. It commandeers my logical mind, and I will do anything to avoid the immediate situation in the store.

All of this is a by-product of my machinery's taking over the controls and my being run by my Organizing Principles. By behaving this way I have betrayed my feelings and values and I have deprived my child of a responsible parental response—and I have the guilt of knowing that I've done this, to myself and to my child.

My Organizing Principle "I must stay in control" is one of my most harmful. I now know that I can't control anything except the choice to be conscious and to make conscious choices. Still, my machinery can't stand the feeling of being "out of control" and seeks to be "in control" so it can insulate itself from the actions or feelings that it judges to be dangerous. My machinery "feels safe" when I'm "in control," even though being in control is an illusion, just that old armor to be tripped on over and over again.

My machinery's Organizing Principle "If the people I really love really loved me, they would not put me in a terrible position" is another iteration of past pain that keeps me in a loop, denying possibilities and keeping me re-experiencing the very same past pain that it's trying to avoid. How can anyone, no matter how close to me, possibly anticipate everything I would want without my telling them? This Organizing Principle actually functions as a test that, at least sometimes, they are bound to fail. When they fail, it validates another of my Organizing Principles: "No one will take care of my needs but me." I can't imagine a more airtight system of beliefs for insuring that I would feel on my own and alone.

This is why, as I'll discuss in chapter 11, we have to learn new principles that will help us create more fulfilling lives instead of being guided by our old Organizing Principles that kill off possibilities and so often keep us frustrated. But first let's look at Jung's illuminating way of understanding the area of our inner world that our defenses keep us from seeing. We need to become aware of how this part works in order to make conscious choices about our behavior.

CHAPTER TEN
BECOMING AWARE OF OUR DARK SIDE AND LEARNING TO EMBRACE IT

As we know, in terms of how our mind works, we have a conscious mind and an unconscious mind. Jung sees the unconscious mind as composed of two parts: the personal unconscious and the collective unconscious. The personal unconscious contains the specific parts of ourselves as individuals that our conscious mind—what we think of as "I" or "me"—finds unacceptable because they clash with our expectations of ourselves from childhood experiences of what we think to be "good" or "bad" behavior. The collective unconscious contains the archetypes, processes, and other information inherited at birth and common to all human beings, including our connectedness to the Higher Power.

Jung also calls the personal unconscious the shadow aspect or dark side. I like these terms because they emphasize that the authentic parts of ourselves that the conscious mind has hidden are actually banished into the shadows, where they continue to function without our seeing them. Our dark side contains our self-defeating programming, including our complexes. It contains repressed memories that we deny because our conscious mind doesn't want to deal with them. And, as you'll see, the dark side also contains some of our emotions that our conscious mind finds too difficult or painful to deal with.[1]

According to Jung, the less conscious we are of our dark side, the blacker and denser it becomes. This is because, when we keep these banished parts of ourselves out of our conscious mind, we cannot have the opportunity to consciously work with them or use them constructively. But when we consciously begin to become aware of these despised parts, through looking at our interactions with others and at our dreams, which can tell us a lot about what we are hiding about ourselves, we can begin to embrace the parts of ourselves that we have denied and we can become whole and authentic.

When we embrace our dark side, we can modify the behaviors and thoughts that our machinery has judged negatively and we can use them for a positive benefit. Jung spelled out what these benefits are: Integrating the shadow vitalizes our personality. It allows normal instincts, appropriate reactions, realistic insights, and creative impulses to take their natural place in our behavior. By our embracing our dark side, Jung said that the carbon turns into a diamond.[2]

I described one of my machinery's strategies for getting rid of my feelings as "splitting them off" and noted that one of the feelings I disowned was my anger. I came to understand that these emotions then lived in my dark side. For many years, I split them off so completely that I didn't even believe they existed.

We split off our dark side from our conscious mind because our machinery's programming believes that these parts of us are incompatible with how we should present ourselves to the outer world and therefore can't tolerate them. Regarding anger, for example, my self-image required that I see myself as a hero, like

Luke Skywalker in *Star Wars*, like the hero I had wanted to be to my mother when I was a child, feeling I had to take the place of my father. I couldn't tolerate the thought that I could have a Darth Vader side capable of blowing people away with my anger and hostility if it got out of control. Put in terms of my programming, my persona says that I'm a nice guy who would never intentionally hurt anyone, so how could I possibly ever be angry, let alone be filled with rage?

We all have a dark side, and the more we remain unconscious of it, the less we see the destruction it's causing us and others in our lives. The specifics of what is banished to our dark side vary for each of us: Which parts of ourselves are hidden there depends on what our machinery judges to be unacceptable to the outer world. It's not always anger that's banished to the dark side. For a man with a "tough guy" image, his machinery may banish his "nice guy" qualities into the dark side for fear of appearing weak.

There's another aspect of us that determines what is relegated to the dark side, and it has to do with how we orient ourselves and function in the world. Jung says that there are four functions of our psychic selves: thinking, feeling, intuition, and sensation.[3]

Thinking and feeling are, in Jung's terms, logical or rational functions because they are reflective. Thinking is the mental process of interpreting by reflection what is perceived. Feeling is the subjective function of reflection that evaluates or judges what something is worth. Intuition and sensation are irrational functions because they don't depend on logic or reflection. They are both ways of perceiving what is: Sensation perceives the details of the physical world. Intuition, which springs from the world of imagination, picks up what is in the inner world and also has hunches about possibilities in the physical world.[4]

How we personally use these functions is influenced in part by whether we are extroverts or introverts. For each of us, either thinking, feeling, sensation, or intuition tends to dominate the way we observe and respond. If thinking is dominant and is our primary way of functioning in the world, then its opposite function, feeling, is relegated to the shadow side, where it is less developed, while the other two functions (sensation and intuition) are more accessible to us.[5]

Even though our machinery splits off and hides parts of us in the dark side so that we're not aware of them, they still influence our behavior, only we don't necessarily see it.

It's like letting out gas. Nobody likes to admit that we let out gas, but if we eat gaseous foods, the gas is inside of us and has to come out. If it didn't come out and instead stayed inside, it would become toxic.

"Freudian slips"—the words that pop out that we consciously don't mean to say but that reveal how we truly feel—generally come from the dark side. A vivid example of a Freudian slip was provided by a woman writing to an advice columnist about a letter she received from her daughter-in-law that began, "Dead Mother-in-law" instead of "Dear Mother-in-law." The woman said that although she knew the "d" and "r" are near each other on the keyboard, she felt this was a Freudian slip that showed her daughter-in-law's hostility toward her, which the mother-in-law had always felt under the surface of her daughter-in-law's behavior.

Think of it this way: *Whether you are conscious of something or you're not, the unconscious knows. What you don't become aware of comes out in your behavior and you get it as your destiny!*

For example, if someone is victimized in his family system and doesn't acknowledge or resolve this, then his destiny is intertwined with victimization (either as victim or victimizer) his whole life.

Sometimes others can help us get in touch with our dark side. If there's someone you instinctively just can't stand, that person may be mirroring for you the parts of yourself that you've banished to the dark side and that you need to bring into the light and to integrate into yourself. I think of these people as my gurus or teachers.

For example, when we meet someone whose arrogance drives us up a wall, it's because we unconsciously hate that part of ourselves. Indeed, our machinery may even interpret appropriate pride in our accomplishments as arrogance if our programming says it's not all right to be proud because it would give us a swelled head. If we've relegated appropriate pride to our dark side, when someone displays appropriate pride we will see it as arrogance and it will irritate us.

If your thinking function is your primary way of reflecting on what you encounter, you may be annoyed by someone who responds to the world primarily from the feeling function, which is subjective. When your thinking is dominant, you have all sorts of reasons for and ideas about why you're responding as you are, and interacting with a person whose feeling function is dominant, you may be irritated by his or her lack of reasons and ideas.

If you're aware that your irritation is prompted by the other person's mirroring what you've unconsciously consigned to your dark side, you recognize that your irritation is not an appropriate reaction to the other person but rather that your machinery is being activated by something within you that you have not yet acknowledged or accessed.

<hr>

Pause Your Machinery

Write your responses to the following:

- Identify yourself as either an introvert or extrovert using a scale of 1 to 10, with 1 being Extremely Introverted and 10 being Extremely Extroverted. It's possible that you've never thought about this before. Describe any insight this gives you into your personality or behavior.

- Describe whether you base most of your decisions through thinking or through feeling. For example, are your decisions based on a careful analysis of the facts or on how you feel about the situation?

- Identify and describe an instance when you felt that someone else was reacting to a situation in a way that made you uncomfortable or that you judged critically. What was their mode of response? For example, was it anger, avoidance, direct attack?

- Is this a way of behaving that you consciously tend to avoid? Summarize what it is about this behavior that makes you uncomfortable or makes you judge it critically.
- Can you recall a recent incident where this behavior "slipped" out of you? How did that occurrence make you feel? Did you judge yourself critically for it? Or, did you split it off so entirely into your dark side that you were unaware of it until someone else pointed it out to you?

Recognizing that my dark side exists and knowing some of what I have hidden there has helped me to begin to see what I was doing in my behavior that damaged my relationships. My pain eased as I began to be more trustful of myself. Instead of fighting off my dark side, I started to be aware of it and to accept it.

When I began to experience that I had a dark side, I started to recognize that I could and sometimes did act out in angry ways and then erased all memory of those actions. I began to see that my machinery could split off what I consider "bad behavior" as if I never did it. Recognizing this allowed me to understand situations that formerly didn't make sense to me, situations in which I had unconsciously acted angrily and when people had told me I had acted angrily, I didn't believe them.

Splitting my anger off into my dark side deprived me of my power. I unconsciously felt like a wounded elephant holding his anger in because he was afraid that if he let it out he couldn't help himself from trampling those around him, so to protect the others, I punished, victimized, enslaved, verbally battered, and shamed myself for the rage I couldn't admit was in me.

If people accused me of being angry, I would deny it and perhaps attack them. I kept the elephant in various prison cells and gave the keys to those closest to me and told myself that it was they who were my jailers, that it was their fault I was containing the anger I wouldn't admit I had. Of course this only made me angrier!

I would shut down because I felt guilty over my anger and was afraid that if I felt it, I would blow up. All of this eliminated any chance for true emotional intimacy with the people closest to me. How can you be emotionally intimate with anyone when you're trying to hide your emotions?

I began to have more compassion for myself as I started to recognize my anger and to understand that it came from the old hurt and pain that I had not been willing to own. I started to see that I had been carrying around what the therapist called "murderous rage," most of which related to my long-dead father for leaving me, and how that rage would come out from my dark side without my being aware of it.

These recognitions allowed me to realize why I hated having confrontations with the people closest to me: Unconsciously I had been afraid that my murderous rage would make me the Darth Vader I never wanted to be. More fundamentally, I was scared that the rage would come out in their direction, which would result in making them abandon me.

I learned that my inability to acknowledge and embrace this anger that came from my old hurts and pain forced me to keep my appropriate anger in my dark side, too, so that I was unable to own and express it. Once I recognized and began to access and feel the anger that I had been hiding in my dark side, it allowed a more vulnerable, spiritual side to emerge in me. The more I acknowledged my hidden feelings, the more comfortable I was and the more comfortable my relationships became for all concerned.

I'm sharing this because, as Jung emphasized, all of us hide our dark side from ourselves, and I'm hoping that my experience will help you begin to access the parts of yourself that you may be hiding in your dark side. Remember, by embracing and incorporating these hidden parts, we become the unique, authentic individuals we truly are. When we embrace our dark side, we are no longer at the mercy of its coming out unconsciously; we are able to act consciously and constructively.

Anger as a Cover for Pain and Fear

I mentioned that I'd been hiding pain from old traumas in my dark side. Part of what I've discovered is that sometimes when we're angry or experiencing another intense emotion that anger or other emotion is actually a cover and a defense for feelings that we unconsciously find even more unacceptable, such as pain or fear of losing someone we love. Unresolved pain can turn into rage, as it did for me. Our Organizing Principles are intended to keep us from becoming aware of this.

I didn't just split off my anger and pain; sometimes I split off my fear, too. As with anger, splitting off our fears doesn't mean they go away; it just means they are repressed from our consciousness. They still continue to play a significant part in how we act. I began to see that my biggest fear was abandonment and that I had split off this fear into my dark side, too.

For years, I had no idea that my machinery was constantly basing its decisions on my fear of being abandoned again! Remember, not acknowledging and not feeling our feelings keeps us stuck in letting them run us! They continue to hurt us and our relationships with others. But, as Jung said, if we embrace our shadow or dark side by getting to know, acknowledge, and feel what we have hidden there, which is a legitimate part of ourselves, we become whole and the carbon turns into a diamond. He also put it this way: "One does not become enlightened by imagining figures of light, but by making the darkness conscious."[6]

Remember, whether you are conscious of something or you're not, the unconscious knows: *What you don't become aware of comes out in your behavior and you get as your destiny!* If we don't understand that we deeply fear abandonment, the programming that this fear creates in us can result in our behaving in ways that invite rejection, which we will experience as abandonment.

PART III

TRANSFORMING
OUR BELIEFS,
OURSELVES, AND OUR
RELATIONSHIPS

CHAPTER ELEVEN

GUIDING PRINCIPLES:
TRUTHS THAT HELP US TRANSFORM

We have the power to replace or supplement our dysfunctional Organizing Principles—and thereby interrupt our programming and fight our complexes—with new Guiding Principles. These Guiding Principles can help us create the future we want for ourselves by allowing us to consciously choose actions that are not past based and that allow for new possibilities that create aliveness and joy. They allow us to become good parents to ourselves, giving ourselves the guidance, support, and nurturance we need to become the people we want to be.

I use the following Guiding Principles to help me move into the now. I've made them my mantra:

1. The truth is just the truth.

2. Feelings are not facts.

3. You can't argue with another's perceptions.

4. Conflicting feelings can co-exist peacefully until they are coupled with actions.

5. Every time something new happens, I go back to my old ways —and I need to snap out of it.

6. Don't do unto others what you wouldn't have them do unto you.

7. Don't stay with familiar pain out of fear of awkward or un-known pain.

8. We can put our bad feelings into others, just as they can put theirs into us.

9. Life is lived in the little things.

Here's how these Guiding Principles work to open my life to unlimited potential.

The Truth Is Just the Truth

I used to be in a terrible bind when I had to be direct with my loved ones if I believed they wouldn't like what I had to say. I was afraid that if I clearly stated my thoughts and feelings I would hurt and inflame them and cause a war, so I dodged and manipulated around anything I felt could be dangerous. By doing this I lost my freedom to fully express myself and thus my power, and my unexpressed feelings turned into anger and rage. That anger and rage got split off into my dark side to remain hidden in the shadows along with the programming that caused me to hide it there. As a result, I was in a continual state of low-level anxiety, with my defenses on constant alert.

Since then I've learned that if the truth is said in a way that is not slanted, if it is stated accurately and without judgment, then "the truth is just the truth" and it is both necessary and appropriate to take a chance and put the truth out there instead of holding it back. I've found that if it is expressed accurately and without judgment, it has incredible power. This has freed me.

Telling the truth gives us access to aliveness. Whenever we're fearless, we're at our best. By not expressing ourselves, we are killing off the potential for change. What we resist will persist. "The truth is just the truth" is closely related to my next two Guiding Principles.

Feelings Are Not Facts and You Can't Argue with Another's Perceptions

"Feelings are not facts" is one of the most powerful Guiding Principles I know for creating the freedom to express ourselves in our relationships. I had a therapist who responded to my stories (which were generally about my being "right" and the other "wrong") by telling me, "Feelings aren't facts." It took years for me to understand what he really meant. Eventually, I got it: He was saying that no matter how strongly I felt something, it wasn't a fact, but only a feeling. It was only my interpretation and often it was inaccurate.

Before I saw this, my inner world went to war over feelings because to me they felt like facts! I didn't know the difference. For me, everything was black and white, right or wrong, yes or no, my way or the highway, and all with intense emotion behind it. As soon as I understood that feelings are not facts, life opened up. I didn't feel I had to go to war anymore!

Life became more comfortable. I could express my feelings as feelings—as simply the truth about how I felt. In other words, I could see that my experience might be different from your experience but it is still the truth about my experience and, although it may not hold for you, it is true for me.

When I state my experience, if I am guided by "the truth is just the truth," I will do it accurately and without judgment. This opens the door for real communication about different perceptions of what happened rather than creating an emotional stand-off in which all that occurs is my machinery battling the other person's machinery.

When it's my machinery versus your machinery, neither person can really hear the other. When there's a difference in perception and one party says, "It's black," and the other says, "It's white," and each insists the other is wrong, it's hard if not impossible for either to bring the other to his or her point of view because each is in his or her own closed system.

When both remember that "the truth is just the truth," "feelings are not facts," and "you can't argue with another's perceptions"—when both remember that they are expressing their beliefs and that both have a right to their beliefs—both can move off their points of view into the present, where they can have a truly open and fruitful debate, resolve conflict, and grow in understanding and intimacy.

Conflicting Feelings Can Co-Exist Peacefully Until They Are Coupled with Actions

A companion to "feelings are not facts" and "you can't argue with another's perceptions" is the Guiding Principle that "conflicting feelings can co-exist peacefully until action is attached to them." As long as actions are not attached to opposing feelings, a situation might be uncomfortable but it will be bearable.

The problem comes when the feelings burst into behavior in which the two people's machinery goes to war. A prime example of this is when two people are angry at each other and one of them attaches an action to his feelings by punching the other in the jaw. As long as we don't attach actions to our conflicting feelings, we hold out the potential for creating the opportunity to talk about our feelings accurately and without judgment while remembering that feelings are feelings, not facts!

Every Time Something New Happens, I Go Back to My Old Ways—and I Need to Snap Out of It

Being aware that "every time something new happens, I go back to my old ways" alerts me to the fact that if I don't interrupt my machinery and become conscious, I will return to old patterns when something new comes up. "Something new" doesn't literally mean something new but instead a new encounter with an old issue that is a look-alike of a past event that my machinery interprets or misinterprets as a possible new threat.

For example, a perceived insult that comes for no apparent reason is "something new" to my machinery, which instantly reacts to it as a possible new threat. This "something new" triggers the same old pattern: It activates my machinery, which then commandeers the driver's seat again. And I am unaware that this is happening! It catches my inner world off guard, and my inner world uses old reflexes to defend against the same old demons—even though this response may not be in my best interest.

When this happens, I'm on automatic pilot. It's as if my inner world hijacks the part of my intellectual mind that has come to know better. Remember: The machinery doesn't care if what it's doing is good for your being or not! When this happens, it's just another example of my tripping over the same old armor without being aware that I've fallen back into these patterns. I'm no longer in the present but have been captured by my past-based inner world, which, for the moment, has trashed all my transformation until I get conscious and present and thereby interrupt it.

I think of interrupting our machinery as analogous to exchanging an automatic shift to a manual shift in a car. In terms of awareness, manual means consciously taking over the controls so that we are in the moment and making conscious choices that drive our behavior. By consciously changing from automatic to manual and bringing to my awareness the Guiding Principle that "every time something new happens, I go back to my old ways," I can short-circuit my old patterns and bring myself into the present, where the chance for new experiences exists and I am not stuck in emotional pain.

Don't Do unto Others What You Wouldn't Want Them to Do unto You

One of my old life-shaping beliefs, which became one of my dysfunctional Organizing Principles, came from a favorite childhood book about the Golden Rule that my dad read to me. My child's machinery believed this "rule" should govern my life and it became law to me. Over time it became more and more of an invisible burden. I didn't realize that I had translated "Do unto others as you would have them do unto you" as my having a personal responsibility to take care of others.

That programming caused me unconsciously to take responsibility for other people's problems. When people I cared for told me their problems, I felt compelled to jump in and help solve them. I had no clue that many of those people didn't ask for my help and may not even have wanted it. Sometimes I would take on their burdens at the expense of my own needs, and later I might become angry at them when I felt they were "ungrateful" even though it was my own fault for taking on the responsibility in the first place!

Eventually I learned that not only had I misinterpreted the Golden Rule because of my programming, I was also incorrect about what the Golden Rule actually is. I'd always thought it was "Do unto others as you would have them do unto you;" then Rabbi Dr. Ron Levine taught me that the statement in the Talmud was "Don't do unto others what you would not want them to do unto you."[1]

Now that I understand the true Golden Rule, my burden of

responsibility has been lightened. It has freed me from my interpretation that I was obligated to help even if I wasn't asked to do so. I realized that I don't need to fill every need I see or even to do everything asked of me. I just have to do my best to make sure that my actions don't hurt anyone. This makes giving a matter of choice, not of duty. It allows me the right to say "No" to someone when I feel the appropriate answer to a request is "No." It makes being generous something I'm pleased to do rather than an obligation that may not give me pleasure.

Don't Stay in Familiar Pain Out of Fear of Awkward or Unknown Pain

Operating under my Organizing Principle "Avoid rejection and abandonment; don't risk losing the love attachment bond," I put up with painful emotional situations for years because I wasn't willing to take the risk that I might not survive the potential pain of going into uncharted territory in a relationship or, even scarier, doing something I believed would lead to the death of the relationship. Afraid of the potential consequences of truly dealing with many problems, I just let them fester by rationalizing that nothing is perfect.

This is the dilemma of familiar pain versus awkward pain; it is survival versus change: the fear of the unknown. Change is frightening, especially when we believe we can survive in the familiar painful situation.

My fear of awkward pain kept me in dysfunctional relationships with little chance of movement in them. Adopting the Guiding Principle "Don't avoid awkward pain in favor of familiar pain" has allowed me the strength to deal with my problems rather than enduring them. It has allowed me to be present in my relationships, open to experiencing what is actually occurring in the now, with all the potential it holds, instead of simply repeating the past again and again and again.

113

We Can Put Our Bad Feelings into Others, Just as They Can Put Theirs into Us

How often have you had the experience that you were feeling fine when you entered a conversation, then the other person expressed his or her negative feelings (perhaps shaming or blaming you), and you walked away feeling awful? Or the opposite experience: You came into a conversation feeling upset, you expressed your negative feelings, and you walked away feeling better?

In the first instance, the other person has put his or her bad feelings into you and now you're stuck with them; in the second, you've put your bad feelings into him or her. It's like the child's game of tag, where one kid touches the next and says, "You're it," and the tagger is now free while the one who was tagged has to find someone else to take his burden from him.

When we put our bad feelings into others or they put theirs into us—making such statements as "You did this to me" or "It's your fault that I _____," we no longer have to take responsibility for our feelings; we put that responsibility on the other. It's like we are using the other person as a trash container.

We build this system in childhood. Little kids get hurt and want their parents to take the hurt away, and their parents say, "Oh, that's okay, Mommy's going to kiss it and make it better." Nobody wants bad feelings; we all want to get rid of them.

When we transfer our negativity, it's sometimes called "dumping."

When our machinery takes over and we give our bad feelings to others or we accept their bad feelings into us, we are acting unconsciously. The more we are aware of this phenomenon, the more we can stop ourselves from doing it.

Life Is Lived in the Little Things

I once heard an author talking about her book of deathbed "exit interviews." Each terminal patient was asked to share what he or she felt were his or her best moments. The answers were amazingly similar. All shared cherished memories of everyday events with the people they loved, such as holding hands during a walk with a grandchild—small, loving moments. It seemed that the only things that had really mattered to these people were little pleasures. There was no talk of the major business deals of their lives, and the biggest problems went forgotten, just as their biggest "accomplishments" took a backseat to simple pleasant memories. To me, this is an incredibly valuable Guiding Principle!

CHAPTER TWELVE
HOW THE MACHINERY FIGHTS CHANGE

We've looked at examples of the Organizing Principles that can run our lives when we're on automatic pilot and of Guiding Principles we can use to replace and supplement them when we make the commitment to transform ourselves in the areas where we feel our programming is dysfunctional. Now we'll examine more closely how we may resist making this commitment and why we may let our Organizing Principles run us even though they frequently lead to self-defeating behavior.

First, a quick review. On the one hand, we know that being run by our machinery costs us the ability to be in the moment along with love, affinity, freedom of expression, satisfaction, fulfillment, vitality, and well-being. We also know that when we are being run by our machinery we can't stand to look bad, and, therefore, almost everything we say and do during that time has the goal of justifying ourselves and making others wrong. These are the illusory rewards of being run by our machinery.

Intellectually we can compare these ostensible rewards with the costs and realize that they pale in comparison. We know, intellectually, that these "rewards" are really our defenses, keeping us in the past and killing off any chance for new and more fulfilling experiences. But that still doesn't mean that we're going to make the conscious effort to interrupt our programming. Why?

A major reason is fear: all the fears that make us desire to be right and to make others wrong, to dominate or avoid being dominated, to justify ourselves or invalidate others—these are all ways that our machinery says makes us feel the tribe will validate and accept us. We are afraid of letting go of our set ways of presenting ourselves because we are afraid of being vulnerable, afraid of unfamiliar pain, afraid of the feelings we are repressing. It's our fear—often unconscious fear—that makes us hold on to beliefs that intellectually we know are disruptive to our lives.

We have to become aware of this fear and how our programming triggers it in certain situations so that we don't allow the fear to control us. We must also focus on the fact that continuing to act in ways that our Organizing Principles dictate reinforces our machinery and our set ways of presenting ourselves. The more we allow this, the stronger our programming becomes and the more we believe our set way of presenting ourselves is who we are.

It's a self-defeating cycle: Our set way of presenting ourselves is entrenched in the belief that we must defend our actions and our point of view; our point of view determines our actions; our actions bolster our set way of presenting ourselves and function as part of our machinery's defense system.

The payoff of this programming is that it creates a temporary situation that makes our machinery "feel good" or "feel safe"—but, as we know, it's at the expense of letting information in that will allow change and thereby interrupt the machinery or, in Jungian terms, that will help us to dismantle our complexes brick by brick. It's at the expense of being in the present and feeling our feelings.

We confuse the illusory and temporary payoffs of our programming as being the only payoffs available to us. Until we make the commitment to transform ourselves, we stay stuck in the self with a small "s" and lose sight of our being; we lose sight of even the potential for something truly better. The longer we let our machinery run us, the more habituated we become to it. It's like learning to stand in sewage without even smelling it anymore.

As I started to see how my Organizing Principles were running me on automatic pilot, I started seeing the mistaken payoff from believing that the suffering I experienced in my close personal relationships was acceptable because "suffering is just part of life." I also started seeing that continuing to suffer just reinforced this belief. I started seeing, as well, that I had been putting up with suffering because it was familiar pain and I was afraid of unfamiliar pain and of potential abandonment. Again, this was a vicious cycle.

My belief that the pain was inevitable was a rationalization for enduring it, and the risk of what it would require to move beyond it was too threatening for me to take the necessary step of making choices to break the pattern. And of course there were the temporary payoffs that at the time I mistook for real payoffs. By enduring pain in my marriage, for example—my closest relationship—I got the temporary payoffs of not having to deal with my fear of abandonment and of justifying myself and invalidating my wife.

We can't become good partners in a relationship, or become good parents to ourselves, let alone good parents to our children, until we do the conscious work to transform ourselves. Yes, it does take work to become and remain aware of our programming and, yes, we do have to back up our awareness with our will to transform ourselves in order to interrupt our machinery and make conscious choices. Every time you find yourself wavering and falling back into old self-defeating ways, remind yourself that the costs of continuing to operate with that old programming are far greater than its temporary payoff!

Pause Your Machinery

Write your responses to the following:

- Identify the last time you reacted automatically based on one of your Organizing Principles. For example, perhaps you snapped at a loved one because of your Organizing Principle "If someone doesn't agree with me, they're rejecting me," or perhaps you chose not to confide in a friend when you had the opportunity because of your Organizing Principle "It's not safe to tell others my real feelings, because they won't understand them." Describe the incident as well as the Organizing Principle it relates to.

- Describe how you felt immediately after the event. Did you feel relief? Satisfaction? Did you feel in control? Or a sense of frustration?

- Describe how you felt a day later. Then describe how you felt several days later. Did your initial response turn into something less positive? Did you even come to regret your actions or feel out of control?

Now it's time to see what we can do to tip ourselves off that we're acting on automatic pilot and look at a technique for switching from automatic to manual so that our choices become conscious ones.

CHAPTER THIRTEEN

RECOGNIZING WHEN WE'RE BEING KIDNAPPED BY OUR MACHINERY:
CLUES THAT WE'RE REACTING UNCONSCIOUSLY

If you're unconscious, how do you know you're unconscious? I've learned that there are clues that tell us that we're being controlled by our machinery's programming. These clues include

- Swallowing or tightening of the throat
- Holding our breath
- Tightening in our chest
- Experiencing a loss of energy; going unconscious
- Inability to focus
- Starting to use humor, especially humor with an edge
- Knowing that we are RIGHT!

When we see any of these signs in ourselves, it's probable that our machinery is kidnapping our being and that what we are doing is triggered by the machinery's response to a current experience that it associates with a past event. It's also possible that our response may be hiding our fear from our conscious mind.

Some of these clues are physical sensations, generally caused by a form of anxiety that the machinery uses to push down emotions or feelings that it doesn't want to experience. Every time my throat tightens or I take deep, sighing breaths, swallow hard, feel tightening in my chest, hold my breath for no apparent reason, or feel like I'm falling asleep, I know that a complex is taking over.

Pause Your Machinery

As soon as you notice any of these "tics" and realize your machinery has taken over, try this technique that I use to switch from automatic pilot to "manual."

1. Start to monitor your internal dialogue for misinterpretation and misinformation. Even though nothing may objectively be wrong, as long as you're allowing the complex to control you, you will be responding as if something is wrong and you will be responding inappropriately. This awareness is the first step toward being open to your feelings instead of repressing them as signaled by these physical behaviors—your first step toward being in the present, where you can respond appropriately.

2. Take several deep breaths. The most important tool you have when you experience any of these clues is to use your breathing to interrupt the anxiety that is definitely not good for your body. By taking deep breaths, you can consciously open yourself to being aware of your feelings and to expressing them

Losing energy and feeling emotionally heavy is a very noticeable behavioral clue that our machinery has taken over and wants us to shut down. When this happens, we feel drained or tired. This is closely linked with being unable to focus. We struggle to stay awake and can't concentrate. We may change the subject of an uncomfortable conversation or drift into daydreaming. We may experience losing energy and shutting down as collapsing into a state of depression.

The use of humor is a prime clue as well, because we often use humor—particularly sarcasm or distracting humor—as a defense to distance ourselves from our feelings, or to distance ourselves from others or to control them, as part of our machinery's attempt to dominate or avoid being dominated.

One of the biggest clues for me that I've gone unconscious is when I know I'm RIGHT—with capital letters! When I get self-righteous and start announcing to the world how RIGHT I am, it's a sure sign that my machinery is running me! This is also a defense. It's a sign that I'm not using my Guiding Principles but instead that I'm confusing feelings for facts, I'm attaching actions to my feelings that are in conflict with someone else's feelings, and that I'm battling—rather than letting the conflicting feelings coexist—and having a dialogue in which there is disagreement. It's a sign that I'm slanting "the truth" rather than speaking accurately and without judgment. Again, it's my machinery in action, and I'm killing off the potential for new options and experiences!

So in addition to learning to become aware of the payoffs and costs of our machinery running us, we also have to notice when we get stuck in a belief or point of view and to practice letting go and dropping our resistance to hearing the other person. These are the times we benefit from a real dialogue in which each person can speak without fear of war. This means releasing our attachment to how we see what the disagreement is about and finding the potential for a new, healthier solution that will resolve the conflict.

When I catch myself feeling anxious, attacking someone, detaching from someone, inflating myself, or ruminating about something, I've learned that it's useful to pay close attention to the feelings that lie beneath these clues and the behavior that I'm using as a defense. I've found that there are deeper feelings that we are hiding from ourselves and that we need to learn to honor. Denial is my worst enemy when I'm not getting my needs met and I want to cut off my emotional response. By shutting down and staying unconscious, I simply deny that I'm having the emotional response.

I realize now how life-killing denial is! This is my life—it is happening right now—I can't keep my options open and avoid possible abandonment by cutting myself off from knowing and expressing my feelings. I must voice my needs and my feelings if I want my needs to be met.

By putting our machinery's reasoning ahead of our emotional experience, we prevent the calming/self-soothing that would result from fully experiencing our feelings in our body.

Live authentically in the present!

When you notice that your machinery is activated, ask yourself if it's from the present, past, or both, and then experience the feelings. Don't complicate what you are feeling by imposing intellectual cognitive meanings. Comfort comes from feeling our feelings. Soothe yourself by taking deep breaths until the anxious feelings disappear, and then be willing to face the feelings directly and not ignore them or dump them on someone else.

Look within to your deepest and very important feelings; treat your feelings as you want them to be treated: with precision, love, and care. Everything we do should be toward clearing out all the stories in the machinery so that all that is left is our Self, our being.

Whenever I'm fearless, I'm at my best. Being in the now is kryptonite to the machinery. Remember, true opportunity has no shelf life; it only exists in the present. Resignation and cynicism kill life and the potential for miracles.

We start transforming ourselves when we become aware that our machinery is running us. When we have this awareness, and we begin to recognize and respond consciously to the clues that our machinery is running us, we can use what we've learned to make conscious choices rather than to stay unconscious and be controlled by our programming.

In the next chapter, we're going to learn more clues that our machinery has taken over and how we can use this knowledge in our process of self-transformation.

CHAPTER FOURTEEN

HOW TO RECOGNIZE THAT WE ARE IN A COMPLEX:
MORE CLUES THAT WE'RE BEING RUN BY OUR PROGRAMMING

We've explored Jung's concept of complexes, the splinter psyches or mini-personalities that are part of our programming and that can take us over and keep us repeating disruptive patterns of behavior. We've looked at some of the behavioral clues—tightening of the throat, deep sighing breaths, swallowing hard, tightening in the chest, holding our breath, going unconscious or our mind's wandering—that can tell us a complex is taking over and that our machinery is running the show. Now we'll look at what triggers complexes and why when we're in one we respond as though something is wrong when objectively it may not be, and what we can do about it.

The Jungian therapist Dr. Melat, whom I mentioned earlier, explains that there are five elements to a complex that we can learn to identify and understand, and that once we do this, we can fight the complex in five places to keep it from running us. These places are:

1. Image
2. Feeling
3. Perception
4. Memory
5. Behavior

According to Dr. Melat, image is the Jungian term for a specific circumstance, situation, or type of relationship, and that a certain image we encounter may "trigger a particular complex and the feelings that result from it. Learning which image activates which complex can help identify the particular complex and alert you to being in a complex." She suggests that we "get to know the images that trigger different complexes, and fight the complexes by knowing ahead of time what may precipitate them."[1] In other words, understanding how a complex was formed in childhood and learning to recognize the image (specific circumstances, situations, or types of relationship) that will activate the complex in us as adults helps us to know the nature of the complex and what kinds of responses it provokes in us.

Dr. Melat's description of how to do this is so clear and concise that I'll share it with you in her words.

> Let's say that you have a father complex that you recognize by its extreme emotional charge and it's based on your negative interpretation that your father was remote, overbearing, and/or authoritarian. Your work is then to recognize the images that trigger it. For example, you might say to yourself, "My father complex may be triggered when I walk into a bank to apply for a loan, have to appear in a courtroom situation, apply for a job, or address any authority figure."[2]

Dr. Melat explains that if you have a mother complex based on, for example, your feeling that your mother was not nurturing enough during your childhood:

> You might come to recognize the images associated with it and say to yourself ahead of time, "My mother complex will be triggered if I perceive I am rejected or treated impersonally by a woman." The image can come from an event or from a dream that triggers the mother complex, leaving you feeling unlovable. If we analyze our dreams, we can sometimes learn to recognize, through them, the types of circumstances, situations, or relationships that activate our complexes. Then we can bring this knowledge into our waking life to help us identify the images or experiences that may have been activating our complexes without our realizing it.[3]

Remember that certain types of relationships may activate a complex. The more intimate the relationship, the more likely it will trigger our complexes. As Jung sees it, this is because the intimacy of these relationships is closest to the intimacy of parent-child relationships. Our intimate relationships are the most likely to activate our past wounds and unrealistic expectations, which activates unconscious energy and old patterns of behavior—that is, our complexes.

Dr. Melat points out that a smell, a taste, a color, a piece of furniture, a song, or even a sound—any sensory experience that resonates with a past event that is associated with our complexes formed in childhood—can trigger the complex.

The feelings provoked by our complexes are always strong. Dr. Melat explains the emotions associated with complexes this way:

> Having a certain strong emotional response to a situation helps you recognize you're in a complex. The feeling is almost always AWFUL. Generally, if you feel awful, you are in a complex. The feelings are familiar because you've felt

these same feelings many times before, and they tend to arise after specific images or events are experienced in everyday life or in dreams. Use the feeling to know you're in a complex. Each complex has its own particular feeling.

For example, a father complex can make you feel inferior intellectually or economically and has a particular accompanying physical feeling; a mother complex can, in many instances, make you feel unlovable or unsafe and has a particular accompanying physical feeling.

Experience the feeling as deeply as you can, observe what you are thinking, believing, and perceiving about yourself or others, so that you will recognize it the next time it takes over your consciousness automatically. This reduces the autonomy of the complex. It loses the power to jump on your back "like a goblin," as Jung describes the feeling.[4]

Dr. Melat explains how being in a complex influences our perception:

While you're in a complex, you tend to perceive the world through the LENS of the complex…DO NOT BELIEVE what you are perceiving and believing about your life, immediate reality, and people when you are feeling awful and in a complex. Acknowledge that your perception, at the present time, is distorted. Do not act on that distorted perception.

For example, a woman at a service counter does not help you with a problem, and you feel that she doesn't like you and that she thinks you are a loser and has singled you out to abuse, that all women are mean and abusive, and so you leave the counter without finishing your transaction. Reality: She and her boyfriend just broke up, she is angry and taking her feelings out on you.

Test your reality—your perception of reality—by questioning whether your awful feeling is a response to the facts or if it's being determined by a complex. Instead of allowing your awful feeling to dominate you, remain aware and engage with people in the moment to see what is actually happening between you and them.[5]

I was surprised to find out that when we're in a complex, it can also influence our memories. Dr. Melat explains how this works:

As mini-personalities, complexes behave with a selective memory. For example, a complex based on experiencing your mother as insufficiently nurturing can cause you to shift your memory so that you will not remember any time in your life when you were nurtured. When in a father complex based on experiencing your father as highly critical, you will not remember any success or accomplishment in your life, or what you do remember will be minimized or negated. All positive memories will be blocked out by the complex.

Do not act on that distorted memory. Remember, a complex is one-sided. To fight it, take the opposite side. If you are in a complex and find yourself thinking that you've accomplished nothing, start listing your accomplishments. Write a resume. Read them back to yourself in black and white.[6]

Lastly, Dr. Melat explains how being in a complex affects our behavior. She observes that when we're being especially defensive—for example, when we know we're RIGHT!—we're in a complex. She emphasizes that complexes cause a variety of behaviors and that as we become aware of our complexes, we become aware of the specific behaviors they trigger.

Each complex, when active, causes a particular type of behavior. When you know you're in a complex, and you know what your usual behavior is when in that complex, your first line of action, once again, is fighting the complex by doing the opposite of what the complex wants or what your distorted feeling, perception, and memory make you think is appropriate behavior. Going back to the example of the woman at the service counter, don't leave unsatisfied, as that is the complex's behavior (making a drastic change or running away). Instead, do the opposite, stay put, and, again, begin to question what is happening.

Rule of thumb: Never make any major decisions while in a complex! Wait until the awful feelings have subsided, and then contemplate major decisions. Your complex goes wherever you go. It doesn't stay in the house, city, state, job, organization, or with people you leave behind. You will meet it again when an image triggers it. Your only hope is in taking its autonomy away by becoming conscious of how it makes you feel, perceive, remember, and behave.[7]

For me, Dr. Melat's overview on the process of taking apart our complexes is invaluable for its wisdom and encouragement:

It takes time to reclaim the energy bound up in our complexes. Each awful event in our life is another opportunity to reduce our complexes. Welcome them, as they are life-giving opportunities. You must fight the complexes in all five places (image-feeling-perception-memory-behavior). The complex blocks the consciousness just as a wall outside our window blocks our view. You must tear the wall down, brick by brick.[8]

Pause Your Machinery

The next exercise is divided into steps. The first three steps lay the groundwork for identifying and stopping complexes before they take over. The next two steps are the process you will use when you experience a situation or encounter a relationship that starts to trigger a complex.

1. As you go about your daily life, begin to take note of the images (specific circumstances or types of relationships) that trigger your complexes so you can keep them in mind for the future. List these circumstances and types of relationships and write a description of each.

2. Describe the feelings you associate with being in a complex. Remember how you felt when your complex took over and experience those feelings as deeply as you can so that in the future you will recognize them and know that they are being triggered by your complex.

3. Write a list that you can refer to of positive experiences--a résumé of accomplishments--that you can use when a complex starts to take over in order to counterbalance the negative memories.

4. When you encounter a circumstance or relationship that generally triggers a complex, test your perception of reality. Is the way you're responding really a response to the facts or is it your complex?

5. Know that your memories may be distorted. To combat this, refer to your list of positive experiences to counterbalance the negative memories coming to mind as a result of a complex.

Working to Take Apart Our Complexes: What I've Learned about Myself

Like all aspects of our programming that are dysfunctional, complexes lie and are full of falsehoods and inferior thinking. In order to go beyond our complexes, we need to bust them—to confront our complexes with the truth.

Dr. Melat helped me to identify my resistance to transformation and change as my most important problem. There I was, talking to her as my therapist, after years of therapy with others, human potential workshops, and reading everything under the sun about self-transformation, and I was still allowing my complexes to run me; I still resisted change. She commented that I hid so much of myself in my shadow side, denying so many of my feelings, that I was living my life inauthentically. Instead of seeing my own inauthenticity, I saw it in others who demonstrated phony behavior—but I still wouldn't see it in myself.

She helped me to see that my cynicism—my belief that being unhappy in life is just part of life's unavoidable trials and tribulations—along with my unwillingness to fully express my needs and feelings, was not being true to myself, and that I used these beliefs to justify my being stuck.

Seeing this was the start of my confronting my complexes with the truth. One memorable dream image that helped me with this realization was from a dream I had about myself having to wear counterfeit shoes. As we analyzed the dream, I could see that it was showing me that because of my programming, I was walking through life falsely.

Dr. Melat helped me to recognize that my childhood ended the day my father died. I lost it the moment I took responsibility for taking care of my mother, and I was never able to be just a child and be mothered again. From that point, I pushed my feelings aside and denied having them; I was never able to grieve my father's death. My mother—or mother complex—required all of my attention.

I came to understand that when my father died, I lost a sense of being protected by parents. The world was not a very safe place for me. My sense that I had to take care of my mother and achieve for her fueled my anger, which was appropriate, but which I kept in the shadows—in my dark side—fearing to express or even acknowledge it. Dr. Melat helped me to see that in many life situations this prevented me from trusting and from relinquishing control and it disconnected me from my sense of connection to a Higher Power and from the Self that wants me to be whole and loves me for who I really am, and it disconnected me from my feelings.

As a child I shut off the feelings of grief, anger, and longing for love so that I could assume the adult role of my father, which fate left for me to fill. From my childhood perception, I would have been a basket case and of no use to my mother if I let these feelings in; I had to fill my father's shoes, which were impossibly too large for me. This spawned my pattern of pretending adulthood, with none of a child's needs, no matter how much suffering this entailed.

Throughout the decades that followed, I kept committing to my view that suffering was inevitable, and I feared that I was suffering because my faults—my inability to meet my self-imposed expectations—meant that I didn't deserve anything else. My will had become so strong that, despite years of therapy, none of my therapists were able to break down the willful ego I had developed as a wounded child in order to fill my absent father's shoes.

The tenacity of this part of my psyche—the part that was resistant to change and wanted to declare itself a winner while simultaneously living with enormous pain—hung on, no matter what. Only in dreams, Dr. Melat pointed out, when this "willful child" was asleep, did the true Steve—my authentic being—communicate through dream images. But, she asked, would I listen and trust or believe it?

For years, the answer was "No." As I've said, I was resistant—

tenaciously resistant. I was not willing to listen and trust and believe what my being was trying to tell me or what my therapists were trying to tell me. My machinery was so powerful, and I was so invested in it, so terrified of change, that I couldn't hear anything but its beliefs and stories being repeated in my mind again and again, and I couldn't feel anything but the feelings of anxiety and internal conflict that took control of my body and blocked out my being.

I've talked about resistance before. I'm dwelling on this painful part of my history because I want to illustrate how resistance can play out in our lives and to emphasize how very strong it can be. We might think that continuing pain would motivate us to change, but in my case my machinery had a built-in philosophy justifying pain, so continuing pain was not enough, even continuing pain in my marriage.

Complexes always justify themselves; they lead us into the false thinking that we are our complexes and that without them we wouldn't be us. Our complexes make us fear that if we resist them and change our behavior, we won't know who we are. (This is a major part of what tends to keep us stuck in our set way of presenting ourselves.)

Through the anguish I experienced in my second divorce, I finally got that the cost of my machinery's determining my behavior—the cost of remaining on automatic pilot and letting my complexes run me—was greater than the payoffs, and I committed to using the information I had and to gathering more. I was now ready for transformation.

Resistance is inevitable. We all resist. It's part of our programming, therefore part of the human condition. My goal in sharing with you all that I've learned is that you'll be motivated to overcome your resistance and use the tools and techniques this book contains for being more fully alive without having to put yourself through unnecessary pain. Dismantling your complexes and shrinking them down to manageable size may lead you to feeling like a stranger to yourself—but, remember, you are not your complexes, and that stranger you are becoming is your authentic self!

CHAPTER FIFTEEN

BRINGING OURSELVES INTO THE PRESENT: ELEVEN STEPS TO START SELF-TRANSFORMATION

We all have our own core issues that form our programming and reinforce our complexes. These follow us wherever we go—relationship to relationship, job to job, house to house, state to state, country to country—they create pain and defenses that split off our pain and the other parts of ourselves that our machinery wants to deny. All of these factors keep us reliving our past in the present and unintentionally creating our future to be like our past until we learn to transform ourselves, to interrupt our machinery and take our complexes apart brick by brick, and to commit to being in the present.

What power do we have in our arsenal to combat these factors and start our transformation? Awareness. Noticing.

Here's a list of 11 steps you can take to notice your unconscious behavior and become aware instead of letting your machinery and its programming, including your complexes, control you.

———

Pause Your Machinery

1. Notice and reflect on the emotional pain you've experienced over your lifetime, which the machinery interprets and then stores in its stories. Find what could be one of your "biggest" stories. Then, without any judgment, ask yourself in the simplest terms, "What actually occurred?"

2. Notice the patterns you have of reacting to present pain that the machinery judges to be similar to past pain, and notice when these patterns of response don't work to alleviate the pain.

3. Notice your complexes and how, if you allow yourself to remain in them, your behavior and feelings are always the same and they drain your energy. Notice the images (specific circumstances, situations, or types of relationships) that activate the complex and notice the way the complex influences and distorts your perceptions, memories, and behavior.

4. Notice when your machinery is activated and kidnaps your being and you react by repeating old patterns of behavior, that your machinery is reacting to a tale you've told yourself and convinced yourself is the truth. Instead, be aware that it's just a tale that you're telling yourself.

5. Notice when you experience anxiety, sadness, panic, and disappointment, and dialogue with yourself about what caused it. Look to see if it's an appropriate response to a present circumstance or if it's been triggered by a misinterpretation linked to a past event.

6. Notice any situations in which you have gotten comfortable living with the same negative emotional patterns and notice that it's like standing in sewage.

7. Notice how you have adapted, justified, and rationalized "the way life is"—the sign of resignation and cynicism—rather than being present and open to everything that is possible.

8. Notice when you are looking for your happiness from others.

9. Notice how often you go back to an empty well expecting it to contain what you thirst for yet are not getting.

10. Notice how often you seek validation and admiration, and notice that it is caused by programming based on fear and insecurity—and notice how this takes you out of being present in your relationships.

11. Notice that crises become opportunities for self-transformation when you start to interrupt your machinery and make conscious choices.

Noticing is the foundation for self-transformation, and it is a lifelong process. But noticing is only the first step; we also have to use that awareness to interrupt our machinery and make conscious choices. When we do this, we transform ourselves and our relationships. In the next chapter, I'll share with you the lessons I've learned about transforming relationships.

CHAPTER SIXTEEN
TRANSFORMING RELATIONSHIPS

We all want good relationships. The problem is that if our machinery is running us, then it's running our relationships, too, and therefore our future relationships will be similar to our past relationships and will contain the same problems. If our programming creates issues with self-image, trust, intimacy, authority, and/or impulsiveness, these problems will show up in our closest relationships. This is where noticing—awareness—comes in. Once we commit to being aware of how we are interacting in our relationships and to making conscious choices based on our awareness, we can free ourselves from continually recreating our past relationships and bring ourselves and our relationships into the present.

After the breakdown of my second marriage, I recognized that during much of the last few years of our struggle, even though we were both in constant conflict, I hadn't been able to interrupt my programming so that I could actually be present. I saw that, instead, I had spent those years with my machinery's programming being at war with my wife's machinery's programming.

I left my second marriage despite my deep fear of abandonment, even though it meant taking the risk of breaking former patterns. Leaving did not lessen the pain that I felt. In many ways it increased it. But this time I did not run away from the pain or rationalize it. I felt it. The pain I experienced leading up to my divorce and after it served me the way "hitting bottom" serves an alcoholic who finally admits that he or she is an alcoholic and wants to become sober. I'd finally had enough of experiencing the same problems over and over again. I began to face all the real issues and to see the role that I had played in perpetuating the pain. After the divorce, I started to see that if I wanted to have a different kind of relationship, I needed to be different. I felt hungry to reinvent myself and open myself to the potential for fulfillment in relationships.

This is the most fundamental lesson I've learned and it applies to every relationship in our lives: *If we are unhappy with our relationships and want to transform them, we have to transform ourselves.*

Lessons about Relationships

Here are some of the other key lessons I've learned about being conscious in relationships:

- Both partners in a relationship should be more alive because of each other. If we and our partner are not more alive because of each other, we have to take responsibility for our part and figure out what choice to make about it:

  1. Accept the situation totally.

  2. Change the situation.

  3. Remove ourselves from the situation.

- Know that we can each have different perceptions when seeing and experiencing the same things.

- Stop saying, "I know," and instead say, "I feel."

- Be aware that our machinery's major concern is keeping us safe and alive, which leads to a constant need to be validated so that we will be in good stead with our pack, which our programming believes will ensure our survival. Our perceived need to be validated in order to be accepted by the tribe leads to our need to be right, which leads to constantly justifying ourselves, which leads to making others wrong, which is the constant struggle to avoid being controlled, which can lead to controlling others. And all of this is the machinery's process for the sole purpose of keeping us "safe."

- As long as we allow our machinery and its concerns to run us, our relationships will not give us intimacy and nurturing. To transform relationships, put the past in the past; put all the programming's thoughts away—just relate to each other in the present.

- When we go to our automatic setting in a relationship with our machinery in the driver's seat, even though it is familiar and comfortable, it confines us by stopping us from being in the now and by eliminating the potential for new experiences. Once we can identify what our machinery is up to, it has no more power over us and we can invent new possibilities instead of going to our automatic settings.

- The three things that always activate our machinery are
  1. Not getting what we expected
  2. Believing something or someone is keeping us from getting what we want
  3. Not being heard, understood, or accepted by the other person

- We have to have hit bottom in a relationship in order to open the door to genuine positive change, or else we will go on and on operating with the same old programming. More often than not, it takes a crisis before we will truly make a choice about a painful situation.

- If we're perpetually unhappy in a relationship, we have to give up what we're holding on to and take responsibility for our own machinery's causing us to stay in a toxic situation.

- Learn to understand how we project old perceptions from childhood into our current relationships. We may be transferring something that we experienced in our childhood relationships with our mom or dad into a current close relationship (mate, business partner, child, friend). Even though technically we're looking at this person, our machinery stops seeing him or her and instead sees old pain and the person we associate with that old pain, which causes us to act accordingly.

- Once we are aware that our machinery is operating with its old patterns in a relationship, we can interrupt it and reinvent the relationship because we don't have to use our automatic setting anymore. Instead of continuing to suffer and complain, we can accept it totally, change it, or leave it. Remember that if we remain on our automatic setting and don't change it, the relationship will stay the same and our future will look like our past.

- Most people justify their situations by getting allies for the tale they're telling to prove that something is wrong with the relationship. These friends become what I call our "agreement machines." We always know whom to go to for the kind of answers we want. Getting agreement from others for our dysfunctional programming just keeps us acting in the same self-defeating ways.

- Taking responsibility leads to asking, "What did I do or not do that led to what happened?" Doing this gives us power to make conscious choices about how we are behaving in the relationship.

- The battle is between resisting being responsible for our actions and its opposite—making choices and taking action. This will open us up to options that never occurred to us.

- Life works when we take Door #1 or Door #2, and never works when we are paralyzed into inaction.

- Living in a state of complete truthfulness about who we are and adhering to this truth equals power! To whatever degree we sell out this truth, we lose our power.

- We lose power when our promises and agreements are not intact. We lose power when we don't express what we feel. We lose power when we hide or won't state the truth about what's happening in a relationship.

- When something isn't working, it always comes down to our not expressing who we really are, to not being true to ourselves.

- Guilt is a way of deflecting responsibility. If we can't take responsibility for something, it persists. All guilt comes from something that we're keeping silent about. Give up trying to hide something about yourself. Our fear of sharing our true feelings robs us of making a true connection in our relationships!

- All the problems in relationships come from what is not being communicated.

- Anger means there is something to talk about.

- When we argue about money in a relationship, often we are not really arguing about money; money is a metaphor for something more fundamental that we may be afraid to talk about, like not feeling loved or nurtured, or it is a battleground to dominate or avoid being dominated.

- When a relationship isn't working, in order to open the door to potential for change we have to say, "I've had it. This can be no more. All bets are off!" Then we can experience letting go and being in free fall, no matter how uncomfortable it might feel.

- When we are "just being," we are authentic and that is when the world will open up for us.

- Stop trying to fix or manage relationships. Managing relationships—trying to keep them safe, alive, afloat or trying to suppress or hide our true feelings in order to keep the other person from being mad at us—doesn't serve us or the other person. Most of all, it keeps us stuck in the past.

- Instead of trying to fix or manage relationships, recognize that they will turn out exactly as we have constructed them to be, only it may not fit our ideal pictures—but that's not necessarily bad.

- Notice that sometimes we get comfortable living in painful relationships. Recognize that feelings need to take priority—don't use thoughts to push away feelings. Honor your feelings!

- Do not look for your happiness to come from others; do not give them your power.

- If you feel that you are behaving like you're a prisoner, work to free the prisoner! Free yourself! Be authentic. Be present. You're in that prison because you are afraid to fully and honestly express yourself. Express yourself fully. Live without fear and you will have clarity and power.

- Learn to recognize whether you're impulsive and, if you are, what effects your impulsive behavior has on your relationships. When a horse is startled by something, it might bolt and throw off its rider. Sometimes a horse does this because it mistakes a shadow for a snake. The machinery is just like that horse, and when our machinery makes us impulsive, the rider it throws off when it bolts may be our relation-ships. If we don't interrupt our machinery, our impulsive-ness makes us act out, which can kill the situation we were in before we acted out.

- The way we and others talk can kill. Some killers use meat cleavers and some are so subtle that it's like they're mur-dering someone with a butter knife. Language has subtle nuances that can serve as a butter knife. Soft language and sly condescending laughs in a relationship can be used to dominate as effectively as a meat cleaver.

- Often we're not even aware that the butter knife is lacerat-ing us, and we don't notice that our aliveness and joy are being drained. Later we may feel the effects of this without knowing why. Whether someone is using a meat cleaver or a butter knife, it is drawing blood—and we have to learn to notice it and protect ourselves.

- We must also learn to notice when we are killing others through sarcasm, shaming, and blaming. When we no-tice this, we can interrupt our machinery, put away our weapons—whether cleaver or butter knife—and be present to communicate.

- People who activate our irritation, frustration, anger, or any other kind of upset response are often important teachers for us. We tend to think our emotional response is acti-vated because of the other person's behavior and we want to blame them. But the reason people activate us is not their problem, it's ours. If it were their problem, why would we become activated by it?

- Often another person is just mirroring personal traits and feelings that we don't yet recognize in ourselves and that we need to acknowledge. The traits and feelings may be more extreme in the other person, which makes them easier to see, but they only activate us if we share these traits in some form. The reason we don't see this is because we don't like to see ourselves in this way, so we've banished the traits to our shadow or dark side.

- When we recognize this, we can begin observing these traits in ourselves to whatever degree they occur and begin to work with them consciously. Seeing these traits and feelings in others points us to specific areas in ourselves and helps us make the commitment to transform.

Love

Love is a loaded subject for most of us. The reason is our machinery loads it up with interpretations. These interpretations add all sorts of meanings to our human desire for connection and intimacy. I'm not an expert on loving; it's the area where I've had the most to learn and where I still have to put in the most conscious effort to change my perceptions and behavior. Maybe that's why the lessons I've learned about love are so valuable to me. I'll share them with you to supplement what I've shared about relationships.

- Remember that generally it's our machinery that forms notions about love. When we are just being, as opposed to being run by our machinery, there is no right or wrong, loved or not loved; everything is perfect just the way it is.

- The interpretations the machinery adds to love are a trap. They make us believe we need a "love relationship"—often with a particular person—to survive. The only way to get freedom from this trap is to see that our machinery believes that a "love relationship" is an antidote to feeling alone, vulnerable, and worthless—all the things the machinery believes threaten our survival. Telling ourselves that this is just our mind's machinery at work and that it isn't real will take us out of this loop. We must be loving to ourselves and to others and know that survival is not linked to a "love relationship."

- Love comes with complete acceptance after all the interpretations we make up are gone. It's only then that we love a person "warts and all"—the way they are—the good and the bad.

- When we feel hurt or angry in a relationship, often it's because the tales we're telling ourselves about the current situation infuse it with hurt and anger from the past. When this happens, we can change our perception by letting go of the machinery's interpretations. Then we can see the love beneath the gesture and words; we can see the little child, perhaps a wounded little child, inside ourselves and our partner.

- By letting go of the machinery's interpretations, we can recognize that, like ourselves, other people are frequently not conscious of their words and actions, that what they say and do is mostly defensive and not intentionally hurtful. We can recognize that the other person in a relationship may be experiencing our words or actions as an attack even if that's not our conscious intention.

- Stop judging, stop going down the path of critical thinking—shaming and blaming—that takes the responsibility off ourselves. Stop thinking and saying, "If only" the other person would change, instead of telling her or him our feelings. To resolve issues in a relationship, we have to acknowledge that each of us is responsible for what is happening.

- When there are problems in our relationships, we make up our stories and then obsess over what could happen. Instead, we should make up stories we like. The old ones limit us and our possibilities. Our thoughts are the lid of the jar we live in. We can change our mind and remove the lid! Our thoughts are just thoughts—they are not true!

- When we stop judging, love can be found everywhere.
- All intimacy is based on trust.
- True intimacy can only come when the machine turns off and we can resonate being to being.
- In a good scenario, mature love and wisdom replace the attractive image of the beautiful young woman and handsome young man.

CHAPTER SEVENTEEN
RESOURCES YOU CAN USE FOR SELF-TRANSFORMATION

Therapy: A Safe Place to Learn to Feel Our Feelings

As we know, the machinery's defenses often block us from feeling our feelings or even knowing what they are, starting with the feelings we repress in childhood. One of therapy's primary goals is to help us experience our repressed feelings, with a trained, attuned guide. When this happens, it is both healing and powerfully transformative.

The therapist, besides being a co-pilot, provides a safe environment to counteract our fear of our hidden feelings. Once we experience these feelings, we can begin to honor them and make conscious choices instead of allowing ourselves to remain automatically programmed by our machinery.

As Dr. Robin L. Kay puts it, feelings contain energy, and the energy generated by unresolved feelings that come from early trauma prevent us from living in the present and instead keep us at the effect of our machinery.[1] In street talk, this is our "baggage." The job of a skilled therapist is to help us experience our authentic emotions, which are generally complex (pain, rage, guilt, grief, love, longing—often all intertwined with each other). In effective therapy, we learn to tease our emotions apart, identify them, and experience them so that each can be felt individually. When this is properly done, deeply transformative change occurs.

Therapy was the first place I experienced a sense of who I really am. At the time I went to my first therapy session, I had no clue of my machinery's existence. I quickly learned in therapy that my unconscious was a large factor in determining what I did. Gradually I learned how my unconscious worked and became aware of my programming and the complexes that it contained. Most importantly, therapy helped me to heal by helping me feel the emotions I'd hidden from myself.

Therapy also helped me create what psychologists call a coherent autobiographical narrative, a way to describe the unresolved traumas of our childhood, our feelings about them, the coping mechanisms—including our complexes—that arose from them, the self-destructive behavior that resulted from these coping mechanisms, and the feelings that we are now able to get in touch with.

The healing I've experienced in therapy enabled me to write this book and to give you the life examples I've included to explain how our machinery and its programming work. The positive experience I've had in therapy is the reason I recommend it as a valuable resource for self-transformation.

It's been observed that therapy is an art as well as a science. I believe that many of the negative stories we hear about people's experiences with a therapist occur because they've gone to a therapist who is either a bad artist or a bad scientist, or some combination of the two. It's essential to find a therapist with the right skills and the right attunement or "chemistry" for you.

In my experience, in order to have a good feeling about a therapist, the therapist has to be sensitive, non-judgmental, and only have the single agenda of helping you as the patient. Therapy is where I received the good parenting I craved, along with support and nurturance. I still see a therapist and consider it a wonderful luxury supporting my continued growth.

Self-Actualization Workshops:

THE GOOD ONES ARE AN ONGOING RESOURCE FOR INPUT, SUPPORT, AND INSPIRATION FOR MOVEMENT

I've been to many self-actualization workshops and seminars. These workshops have been like the lab courses I attended in high school and college, only the "lab rats" are all of us attending. In the workshops, we observe and learn about ourselves and each other. I attribute some of my greatest personal growth to hearing and seeing others openly discuss their inner lives.

My favorite workshops have been EST, which I took in 1975, and its current counterpart, the Landmark Forum. I spent two weekends in what was then called the EST Training, along with 250 others. As part of the workshop, I heard their stories. I heard them talk openly about things that I secretly, and with great shame, felt and had kept secret in my life, only to learn that these were not uncommon issues and I had nothing to be ashamed of. This was truly the most important six learning days of this lifetime for me. I could never have gotten the same freedom without being there in real time and experiencing the pure truth in that room.

Thirty years later, I took the Landmark Forum and got another healing dose of learning. What follow are some of the valuable life lessons I've learned through these workshops.

How the Machinery Speaks to Us in Words

Everything that exists in our machinery comes up for us in words. The stories and interpretations that keep us in the past are all stated in words. If we give ourselves new stories and interpretations—new words, new language—we transform ourselves and live in the present.

Human beings are the only species that I know of with this kind of language ability and perhaps that is why we have the unique problems that make us human and that do not affect any other species. The way we talk influences the quality of our life. We've seen how our self-defeating programming keeps us in the past, promotes resignation and cynicism, and kills aliveness and potential. Instead, you can change the way you think by changing the words, the language you use, and thereby create the experience you want in your life.

Instead of using the language of past-based limitations, we can use the language of potentiality—of new options, of the capacity to grow. The language of potentiality—or as Landmark calls it, "the language of possibility"—is always in the present or the future. It is simple and makes a declaration; it declares what we can become. Here are some examples of how I use the language of potentiality:

- I am the potentiality of being vulnerable, passionate, open, and in the now.

- I am the potentiality of knowing my own feelings.

- I am the potentiality of being sensitive to other people's feelings and of their being sensitive to mine.

- I am the potentiality of being a strong, clear partner in a loving relationship.

- I am the potentiality of being a strong, clear father to my children.

Potentiality—possibility—exists when we are authentic. When we declare our potential—when we live in possibility—we are in uncharted territory. We are in the land of miracles!

AUTHENTICITY

Being authentic means just being. We never escape the cost and impact of not being authentic. Being authentic about our inauthentic parts—seeing and acknowledging what our machinery is up to and the way it causes us to present ourselves to others—opens new possibilities. Committing to new possibilities brings us into the present. It is what makes us authentic.

We're all looking for validation and admiration. But if we get admiration through deception (inauthenticity), the admiration is based on some form of a lie and it can never bring us a sustainable satisfaction. Authenticity doesn't require admiration or validation because we are just being!

BEING COMPLETE

Most of us know the uneasy feeling when a situation is not fully defined or comfortable, when a problem or disagreement continues unresolved, when a relationship has a crack in it that never seems to mend. These are symptoms of something in that situation not being complete.

Actions that create completion are

- Giving up what we are holding on to (letting go of an old point of view that we are still carrying with us)
- Taking responsibility (accepting that we are choosing to act as we do and feel as we feel instead of blaming others for our actions and feelings)
- Acknowledging (stating what is so for us)
- Forgiving (letting go of old grievances against ourselves and others and approaching the situation with an open heart with new eyes)

We can all take these actions if we choose to do so. Being complete requires being in the present, while being incomplete means we're allowing ourselves to be controlled by our past and our machinery.

GUILT ALWAYS COMES FROM SOMETHING WE'RE AFRAID TO SAY

Another helpful truth I've learned is that guilt comes from unde-livered communication. We feel guilty because we have the per-ception or feeling that we're doing something wrong and keeping silent about it. When we make full disclosure, we are putting everything on the table and there is no longer anything to feel guilty about. Making full disclosure means taking a risk, but holding on to guilt is risky, too, because it blocks our aliveness.

THE THREE THINGS THAT ALWAYS RESULT IN UPSETS

I call situations that cause suffering upsets. Whether upsets are big or small, there are three things that always provoke them—the same three things I mentioned earlier as activating our machinery in relationships:

1. Unfulfilled expectations
2. Thwarted intentions (something or someone is keeping you from getting what you want)
3. Incomplete communication (what you are saying is not heard, understood, or accepted by the other person)

At the heart of Buddhist philosophy is the observation that human suffering is caused by attachment and that avoiding at-tachment means avoiding suffering. Unfulfilled expectations cause upsets because we are attached to our expectations about outcomes. We do something expecting a certain result, and if we don't get it, we are upset. Similarly, we are attached to our inten-tions (to accomplishing what we are determined to do), and if we are prevented from doing these things, we are upset. Lastly, we say something to someone and we are attached to our expectation that what we've said will be heard, absorbed, and accepted, and if it's not, we are upset.

It's very difficult to avoid being attached to our expecta-tions and intentions, but if we keep in mind these three causes of upsets, we can pinpoint for ourselves why a particular upset has occurred and be aware that it is our machinery and its interpretations that are causing the intensity of the upset. In other words, it is our programming, with its fears, its associations with past events, and its "shoulds," that is causing us to be attached and to react with such intense, and often distorted, emotions when we are disappointed.

When we become aware that our machinery and its programming are causing an upset, it's less likely that we will start shaming and blaming others or ourselves for it, and we make it easier to experience whatever feelings arise, move on, and make conscious choices in the present. In other words, instead of being locked into the upset and into our machinery's response to it—instead of getting stuck in suffering—we open ourselves to possibility!

Suffering Lives in the Stories We Tell Ourselves

We experience suffering because of our stories. It's crucial to remember that we make up our stories. If we live in our stories, we live in an unreal world because our stories are full of interpretations (since the machinery mostly hears what it expects to hear and sees what it expects to see instead of processing events in a factual way). When the facts are laid out in their purest form with no interpretation, there is no suffering. Everything is just what it is, and this really isn't good or bad. It's just what happened. It's just so.

Keep in mind that suffering comes from what we make up in our stories. Here's an example of what I mean.

In a workshop I attended, we were asked to state something we were suffering over. After everyone in the workshop had written accounts of our suffering, we paired up and read our story over and over to our partner until we just couldn't do it any longer.

Eventually, each of us got sick of the repetition of our own story and began to understand the concept that suffering lives in the stories. The stories are interpretations. There is really no right or wrong, good or bad to them; they are our interpretation of what happened. What we have to do now is to choose the future we want to live into.

If we have been telling ourselves a tale about our childhood with the interpretation that we have been victimized by our parents' deficiencies and/or external circumstances, instead of staying stuck in this story for the rest of our lives, we can choose to create a new one. We can state the unadorned facts of what happened, love ourselves for who we have become, and recognize that we wouldn't be who we are without having taken our particular journey. We can acknowledge ourselves for taking the journey and be grateful for the lessons we have learned and for having the awareness, the desire, and the will to continue to grow and to transform ourselves. That story gives us a future we want to inhabit!

LIVING A LIFE OF HONOR

Another aspect of self-transformation is that we reinvent ourselves. I believe that we accomplish this by living a life of honor.

To live a life of honor, we need to be authentic—to just be and to live truthfully, adhering to our principles. This is not only about giving one's word and keeping it, nor is it just about always telling the truth. These are very important, but real honor starts with being true to oneself. If we're being false to ourselves, we can have no honor.

Miracles can only show up in our life when we honor ourselves—and we never honor ourselves when we do things for others just to get the world's approval. This is why we have to be aware of our machinery's desire for getting validation and admiration.

It's important to distinguish between honor and our ideas about morality. Often we think, "He did this for me, so I should do that for him," even if we don't feel good about what we would be doing. This is not in alignment with being honorable; it is a "should" that arises out of our concept of what is moral. We must do things because they honor ourselves as well as serve others.

Living a life of honor consists of

1. Doing what we say we will do, and if we change our mind, taking responsibility for the change and expressing what we will do now

2. Telling the truth

3. Being at peace with our thoughts and actions

4. Doing what we know is right, in spite of our fear of possible consequences

Doing what we say we will do means our word can be counted on, that we will keep our agreements and take responsibility if we don't.

Telling the truth means we will communicate accurately and without judgment and act consciously in the moment, making us open to potentiality, to whatever may happen. This means being open to resolving disagreements. We must be straight in our communications and accepting rather than trying to control the responses we get from others.

Being at peace with our thoughts and actions means letting go of our interpretations.

Doing what we know is right, in spite of our fear of possible consequences means acknowledging our fear and going ahead anyway—and making a conscious choice to give up the belief that "There is a terrible problem here." It means behaving as though we're fearless!

For some of us, it takes a lot of courage to fully express ourselves. But when we hold back, we are cutting off the possibility of closeness with other people. We can only create real connections with others through full freedom of expression combined with authenticity. For me, learning this has been the key to having the love and true emotional intimacy that I've always craved and found so difficult to get.

As I've mentioned, it's been easy for me to fully and authentically express my feelings about business deals, but in my personal life full self-expression and authenticity have been scary, and often my fear has shut me down. Again, my machinery's interpretation was that if I told my loved one what I really felt, I would be doing it at the risk of being abandoned. So I didn't risk it. This behavior always led to feelings of emptiness; if you don't ask, you don't get, but my machinery added the interpretation that I was not getting because I was not worthy of getting.

"Unworthy" is an empty concept. The world doesn't care who is or is not worthy. Many people deserve to win the lottery, and yet many people who are not as worthy hold the winning tickets. Deciding whether we're worthy or not is a story we make up, a game that we're playing with ourselves.

Doing what we know is right, in spite of our fear of possible consequences—acknowledging our fears but behaving fearlessly—is the key to being fully alive with a life of honor. We all have many explanations for why we shouldn't, couldn't, or won't do something, but by acting in spite of our fear we are creating a future that is not limited by our past. We are living a life of honor. We open the door to making our lives truer and richer, and to making the planet a better place!

The Four Agreements

Miguel Ruiz, in his book *The Four Agreements*, teaches us to avoid needless suffering by using his four rules. I believe Ruiz's four principles are an elegant and effective way of keeping all interpretations out of our stories and therefore eliminating the suffering we would experience because of interpretations. The four agreements are also guidelines for living a life of honor.

As Ruiz states them, the agreements are

1. Be impeccable with your word.

2. Don't take anything personally.

3. Don't make assumptions.

4. Always do your best.[2]

How Do We Learn to Love Ourselves?

Learning to love ourselves is essential to inventing ourselves anew. The machinery is a notorious self-critic that sometimes leaves us with negative and self-destructive feelings about ourselves. The concept of learning to love myself was so new to me that I found it helpful to keep a list of the ways to love myself that I've found effective.

Although this is my personalized list, I hope you'll find that some of the suggestions I'm making to myself will apply to you, too. After you read it, I recommend writing your own list to spell out specific ways to love yourself:

1. Protect myself from abuse as if I were protecting one of my children from abuse when they were small.

2. Lead an emotionally full and authentic life.

3. Honor myself every day by staying mindful of and connected to my true feelings.

4. Do one thing every day that scares me just a little—random acts of kindness and regular acts of courage.

5. Embrace my own sadness.

As this list emphasizes, learning to love ourselves means learning to experience our emotions and feelings—not just the words or labels that run through our mind, but the actual physical sensations of the feelings in our body. This means asking yourself, "How do I feel my feelings? Where do I feel them? What do they feel like?"

I've begun building up my capacity to notice my feelings and to become aware of when and where I tend to go unconscious (my "dead zone") and to learn to rescue myself and my feelings by not swallowing them, not trying to cut them off. Remember, you can only honor your feelings if you feel them!

I've come to see that the antidote to anxiety, which tends to block our feelings, is to consciously focus on my anxiety and do physical and breathing exercises to alleviate it. Instead of going dead and being taken over by the anxiety generated by my machinery, I pay attention to my anxiety and scan my body for it. I ask myself, "Where am I tense? Is my breathing labored? Am I holding my breath?"

If I am anxious, I look within to find which emotion or emotions are linked to or being covered over by my anxiety. Is it love, anger, guilt, or grief, or the subset of pain and longing? Often I then recognize the complex that has taken me over.

Part of inventing myself anew and learning to love myself is learning to direct my natural soothing resources—resources we all have inside us—toward myself, both the little child in me and the maturing adult. In reinventing myself, I'm learning that it's all right to give myself love, compassion, tenderness, and care—all of which my machinery made off-limits to me. I'm also learning to stay connected to the pride I feel in moving forward with my life and allowing myself peace.

All of this comes back to the central lesson of learning to honor my feelings. It's impossible to be at peace within ourselves or with others if we don't honor our feelings! This is part of becoming good parents to ourselves. If our parents didn't take our feelings seriously when we were children, it is likely to have created an attitude in us where we don't take our own feelings seriously now. As adults, we don't automatically know how to do this; we have to learn how. And we have to do it for ourselves because nobody else is going to do it for us!

Here's the breathing exercise I've found so helpful in alleviating anxiety:

Sitting up straight in a chair or lying down, close your eyes. Breathe in through your mouth to the count of two, hold your breath for two counts, and exhale for four counts. Fill your belly on the inhale and release all the air on the exhale. Repeat this two or three times.

After you're comfortable doing this for a count of two, move up to inhaling for three counts, holding for three, then exhaling for six counts, and eventually move up to inhaling to four counts, holding for four, and exhaling for eight counts. See if you want to increase the counts. Choose the count that works best for you. We are all different.

If you practice this exercise consciously and conscientiously, it will soon become a natural part of your daily routine, and it will keep you relaxed and reduce anxiety when it bubbles up.

You may find yourself resisting the idea of doing the exercise but, remember, it's all part of learning to love yourself! Why would you want to be anxious if there's a way to reduce your anxiety? The answer is that your being doesn't want to be anxious.

Keeping a Journal as a Tool for Self-Transformation

When I completed my first six years of therapy, I decided to keep a journal to take the place of a therapist. It became a way to reflect on and remember what went on in my life. Putting my thoughts and feelings into words about what I experienced each day helped me understand my experiences and gave me perspective on them. This increased my insight into myself.

When I found myself whining over and over in my journal entries about the same thing, I'd get disgusted with myself. How could I have any self-respect knowing I was repeating the same self-defeating moves and creating the same painful results?

I found myself actually dealing with many of these patterns simply as a result of realizing, through the journal, that they were so repetitious. This is a good way to observe that when we are miserable, it is because of our interpretations, because of the tales we tell ourselves about our lives. I'm still writing my daily experiences in the journal, 30 years later.

I also write about the concepts, tools, and techniques that I've gotten in therapy, in workshops, and in life so that I will remember them and remember to apply them. The sheer action of writing them down reinforces my awareness of the transformative information I'm learning and counteracts the machinery's defenses against learning anything new.

I recommend setting aside a few minutes at night to write about what occurred that day. I write in my journal just before going to bed. I start each entry with the day's date and write about the people and events that have affected me and what I feel and think about them. Don't judge your feelings and thoughts, just write them down. If you've learned a valuable lesson that day, record it.

If you're in a painful time in your life, writing and rereading your entries about the day's events becomes a way of soothing and nurturing yourself while at the same time providing you with a way to observe the patterns your machinery is creating that keep you in pain. The act of writing about your experiences of the day and observing your patterns is taking a stand with your machinery. Writing and reading the journal helps to keep us conscious.

To give you an example of how clarifying keeping a journal can be, I'll share with you an aspect of my journal entries that helped me reach a level of awareness about myself.

Many of my journal entries described disagreements with the people closest to me. I realized that through my journaling I was complaining about how I was being treated, and I suddenly saw that my entries about the arguments were being written entirely from my machinery's point of view. I saw the light! My journal showed that up to that point I was feeling shamed and blamed, and every entry defended my point of view—my set way of presenting myself—and I used it to justify my behavior.

Up to that point, I hadn't recognized that while arguing, I'd heard nothing but what my machinery expected to hear and that my main objective was being right.

My journal shows the night I began to recognize this: "I have spent 15 years writing in my journal so my audience can be presented with my 'case' or how 'unfaired against' my life has been. I must want permission or the world to say, 'What a shame, you're a "prince." Keep up the good work.' "

As I gained insight into the ways in which I tended to behave dysfunctionally in my relationships, I recorded them in my journal. These entries are self-awareness reminders. By recording them in our journal, we help ourselves focus our attention on the aspects of our programming that we recognize as self-destructive, and we remind ourselves that we can interrupt this programming and act consciously.

Here are some of my past entries that illustrate this:

- Often when someone gives me information I'm not ready for, I consider it an attack—not a gift or opportunity!

- I don't have enough gradations of gray between black (I'm bad) and white (I'm good). I'm too hard on myself.

- Inside me I am a critic. "I did something bad or wrong." Instead I should be, inside, an explorer who says, "I made a mistake. I wonder why I did that?"

- By needing so much validation or approval, I am putting my happiness in the hands of others!

- If I "take charge," I don't have to feel emotion.

- My way of interpreting what I believe others are, and then telling them, "This is the way you are," undresses them and gets in the way of good relations.

- "Don't assume—ask first." I must always ask a question when I think I know what someone is thinking—not tell them I think I know what they are truly thinking!

- Ask: "Are you upset with me over something or are you upset about something that has nothing to do with me?"

- My tone of voice may unknowingly be so mean and demeaning that it kills communication. And if the therapist didn't beat me over the head with it, I wouldn't have believed how tough I was on my wife! My dark side had a way of hiding it all from my intellectual side.

- False belief: "If it's really good for me, it will be bad for the other."

- I EXTERNALIZE EVERYTHING! When anything bothers me, I put it outside of me. "It isn't my problem," "She/He/They did it." And most often it lands on or with someone else. It's as though I'm saying, "Hey, I'm just a little boy. I want some grown-up capable person to handle this. It's not for a little boy to handle." When the other person asks me verbally, or in some silent or implied way, to do something I don't want to do, I EXTERNALIZE it, pushing it out of my space, and maybe without knowing it, I give off an attitude that pushes people away and/or pushes my stuff onto or into them. This doesn't work in an ongoing relationship. It pisses people off.

- I don't give myself the compassion and self-nurturing I need, and if I did I wouldn't need validation from others before I acted. I NEED TO BE A GOOD FATHER AND NURTURER AND PROTECTOR TO MYSELF.

- One of my problems is that I am blind to my need for re-fueling and insensitive to the needs of others when I need refueling. It pisses a lot of them off, and I have no idea that it's happening, let alone why!

Here are examples of the valuable life lessons I recorded as I came upon them. They are the kinds of universal lessons you can record in your journal as helpful reminder:

- When the unconscious self has us do things that aren't in our best interest, it's like the unconscious is the Global Positioning

System in a car that picks up some incorrect destinations in our formative years and silently keeps taking us to these mistaken destinations and then has us believe a fight is ahead and that we must shoot first and ask questions later.

- The anxiety comes from my unconscious self being in conflict with my conscious self, which puts me in a bind with myself.

- I learned a major lesson that came out of my class with Rabbi Aron. He told the story of a friend saying to him and his small child that he had been in Japan "trying to find myself." The child didn't understand how anyone could be "trying to find" himself. Rabbi Aron explained to his son what his friend meant, using the terms "Me," "Myself," and "I." The "Me" refers to the character that the person is "playing" in this lifetime. The "Myself" is the character's soul. It's like the Me, or the character we play, is our clothing and under the clothing is the soul. The "I" is the Universal Consciousness, that great interwoven universe that we and everyone and everything else is a thread of (what our society calls God and Godliness). Rabbi Aron explained that his friend had gotten lost in his character. When someone is lost in his character, he doesn't feel connected to the Myself, or soul, and the soul wants to reconnect or better connect with the Universal I. When someone tries to find himself, these are the connections that the soul knows it wants to make.

- From *The Art of Living* by the Dalai Lama: Things that can give pleasure may not always be good for you (the rush from gambling, wild sex, drugs, etc.), as opposed to the pleasure from a job well done or love or the completion of something important. To know if the action is worth doing, ask yourself if the act will ultimately get you inner peace.[3]

CHAPTER EIGHTEEN
IDEAS TO LIVE BY

In this concluding chapter I'm going to share with you ideas to live by that I've picked up along the way in therapy, workshops, books, and just plain life. I think of these ideas as ticklers to remind myself of truths that elude me when my machinery is running me.

Some of these ideas counteract our negative programming about ourselves and state the truth of who we are. Others remind us to stay conscious and to be open to new potentialities instead of hanging on to false beliefs and repeating self-destructive patterns. Some will be new to you; others appeared in earlier chapters. All of them are worth remembering and referring to, especially if you find yourself falling into old negative ways of being.

- *I'm whole, flawless, and complete exactly the way I am.*

What a difference this idea about ourselves is from our machinery's constant self-criticism stemming from its mantra that "There is a terrible problem here," "I'm flawed," "I don't fit in," and "I'm doomed to be on my own."

In fact, there is no terrible problem here, you are good enough, you do belong, and you have always been on your own, and that, too, is just as it should be, because that is the nature of being human. This idea is contained in the age-old truths that "We were born alone and we will die alone" and, at the same time, that we are all part of the Infinite, the collective spirit, "God's kingdom." In this sense, while we are all alone, we are never alone when we are in our being; it's only when we are in our machinery that we may feel alone.

Our machinery often judges us as flawed when we think of things we want to change about ourselves. It's at these times that we need to interrupt our machinery, stop the self-judgment, and remind ourselves that although we have the potential to grow, at this very moment we are whole and complete exactly the way we are. You are a whole, flawless, complete you, just as I am a whole, flawless, complete me!

• *My persona is actually my past.*

It's not me in the now; it's not my Self with a capital "S"; it's just the product of my machinery.

This idea is a reminder that what you think of as you—the tales you tell yourself about your life, the characters you play—are just the product of your programming, created by your interpretations of events that happened in your past. Your persona is your set way of presenting yourself to the world, but it is not you, because you are your being!

• *Life is a blank canvas, and we get to choose which pictures we want to paint on it.*

We tend to think of our lives as a painting with all the detail filled in, including the significance we see in our relationships, goals, ambitions, and values. We may recognize that life started out for all of us as a blank canvas and that we had unlimited potential; what we don't recognize is that even though as life went on and

we painted pictures on this canvas based on tales and interpretations, we still have the same unlimited potential we always did!
Life is still a blank canvas on which we can choose which pictures
we want to paint: If we don't like our old interpretations—the
significance that we have chosen to imbue our lives with—we can
make up new ones we like better and fill our canvas with those!

• *Control is illusory.*

Thirty-five years ago, when my first therapist introduced me to this
fact, I argued and argued about it. Gradually I came to understand
that I couldn't really control anything. If I went to my favorite
restaurant with a yearning for their signature dish and I ordered
it, yes, I was in control of my lunch, but, damn, what if they were
out of it? The truth is I couldn't really control it. I tried to control
two wives and four children, and damn if they didn't do what they
were determined to do, no matter how I tried to control them.

I once heard about a Zen teacher who told his students, "It's
easier to ride a horse in the direction it wants to go." Isn't this
true? At the end of the day, the horse weighs a lot more than you
or I do, and it's a lot stronger, so although we may have the illusion
of control over it, damn if it can't do what it wants!

• *Life is flawless exactly as it is. If you don't like the interpretation
you are giving your life through the tale you are telling yourself,
shift your point of view and re-interpret your life by telling a tale
you do like. Remember, we are gods in our own universe!*

When life is going as we hoped or planned, it's easy to accept that it is
flawless exactly as it is. But it's hard to think of life as flawless exactly
the way it is when we don't like what's happening. When this occurs
we need to shift our point of view and create a new way of looking at
our life that makes it more fulfilling exactly as it is.

Regardless of what our life is like, our circumstances are just
the way they are; the fact of their existence makes them flawless
exactly as they are. For each of us, life is flawless exactly as it is for
who we have been up to this moment, and we can look for its les-

son and act accordingly, using the most fulfilling interpretation of our experiences.

This doesn't mean that everything in your life makes you happy. It doesn't mean your life fits your picture of what you think it should be. It doesn't mean you are not facing challenging circumstances that are very different from what you would have ordered.

Since control is an illusion, we may not be able to create the exact circumstances we want, nor can we make people be the way we want them to be—but whatever our circumstances, we can always change our point of view, the tale we're telling ourselves, and give our experiences a new meaning, a different context.

At this moment, our life is a particular way, and that may or may not fit our picture of flawless, but if it doesn't, we can choose to accept that as flawless exactly the way it is, even though it doesn't fit our picture. In other words, we can choose the tale we tell ourselves. This is what I mean by being "gods in our own universe."

While I was writing this book, a man appeared on a television interview who powerfully and inspiringly embodied that how we choose to interpret our circumstances creates our experience of life. This man was Randy Pausch, a 47-year-old husband, father of three young children, and professor at Carnegie Mellon University. In 2006, while in apparently good health, he went to a doctor with a minor complaint and found out that he had pancreatic cancer and about six months to live. Pausch told the interviewer that rather than waste the time he had left being depressed, he chose to be happy.

This reminded me of a concept I once heard, and which I very much believe, that souls can't be damaged, and that when we are born, in essence we buy a lottery ticket for this lifetime, and as a result a certain percentage of people will die of old age in their sleep, others in auto accidents, and others of heart attacks; some people become tycoons, others work as auto mechanics, teachers, nurses, and so on. Viewed from this perspective, then, Pausch got the lottery ticket of dying young from cancer in this lifetime, and how he responded to it moved and deeply impressed me.

In accepting his circumstance, he committed to choosing to experience his remaining life enjoying as much happiness as he could with his family and friends while raising awareness of pancreatic cancer and funds for research. His final lecture at Carnegie Mellon was the basis of his book, *The Last Lecture*. He told the crowd in the university's auditorium, "If I don't seem as depressed or morose as I should be, sorry to disappoint you . . . I don't know how not to have fun. I'm dying and I'm having fun. And I'm going to keep having fun every day I have left. Because there's no other way to play it."[1]

Randy Pausch gave me a real understanding that I am totally responsible for every aspect of my experience of life and that it is all fine if I choose it to be. He died on July 25, 2008.

- *Misery about our lives comes from our interpretations of our experiences. Life is just what happened and what did not happen. Facts are just facts; they are not misery. Misery comes from the way we interpret the facts.*

Changing your experience of life happens when you recognize that you are operating your own life, that no one is doing it to you or for you, and that your future experience doesn't have to be the same as your past. This means interrupting your machinery and not allowing your old programming to control your actions and interpretations.

- *Every day is a new day. Every moment is a new moment in which we can re-invent ourselves and our relationships anew.*

- *We are born with the ability to express ourselves fully, but as our programming develops we are robbed of it. Take the power back!*

- *Fully expressing ourselves requires realizing what's bothering us and accepting it so that we don't have to be in denial about it. If we don't accept responsibility for what bothers us and allow ourselves to express it, it continues to control our behavior and determine our experience of life.*

- *By accepting your life as it is at this very moment, even if it is not as you pictured it would or should be, you regain the power to make new choices and create new results.*

- *My goal: Managing my mind instead of my mind managing me.*

- *Always work to get back to "beginner's mind!"*

Remember when you were very young and everything was new and amazing and full of surprises? That is "beginner's mind."

A "monkey mind" jumps all over the place and is always just the machinery, flitting from thought to thought. Remember, when we see everything through our experience of the past, we're really not seeing it as it actually is. We're only seeing what we expect to see and hearing what we expect to hear. We're not seeing or hearing in the present; we are merely attaching to present events our past pictures of what has happened before.

Because a beginner's mind isn't run by the machinery, it is empty of programming and can receive true impressions of the world. When we've interrupted our machinery and have a beginner's mind, we are not attaching pictures from the past to what we are experiencing. We are in the present!

- *When we have judgments of "right" and "wrong," "good" and "bad," we are not in the present and not able to connect!*

For me, this is a very important and freeing concept. It highlights the fact that when we are labeling "right" and "wrong," "good" and "bad," we are interpreting, we are judging, which means we are being controlled by our programming and its interpretations instead of being in the now. When you find yourself applying these judgments to your experience, it's a sure sign that you need to interrupt your machinery!

- *Pain and suffering are better than being anesthetized. Comfort can only come once we feel our feelings, even the painful ones.*

It's better to feel than not to feel, even if what we are feeling is painful. Remember, pain can be a great motivator to make changes that will ultimately lead to a more fulfilling life!

If you find yourself feeling pain and wishing that you were numb, ask yourself what the pain is telling you about your life. What new choice is the pain asking you to make to interrupt your machinery and transform your experience?

- *Fear makes the wolf appear bigger than it is.*

- *Many fears never go away. The goal is not to become free from fear, but to identify our fears, accept them, and then not be stopped by them.*

- *We're all afraid of each other, so why be afraid of anyone?*

- *When you want to be liked by others, you can't say "No." Instead of automatically saying "Yes," ask yourself, "What would I do if I were not trying to be accepted?"*

- *Be like a strong tree in the forest that doesn't need anyone.*

- *I can only change me. I can't fix or change others; it's not my responsibility and I can't do it even if I want to.*

- *Feeling guilty comes from holding back instead of expressing ourselves fully.*

If we fully express what we feel, we will have no guilt and others will have to make their own decisions about how they are affected by it. It's no longer our secret and, therefore, we will not be controlled by our shame or fear. Doing this requires taking a risk—the risk of being vulnerable in the moment.

- *I'm fascinated with my insights. So what? My insights don't do anything. They only mean something if I commit to acting on them.*

- *Get clear, choose, take a stand, commit, and don't sell out.*

- *Every night our machinery reboots as we sleep, and in the morning we have to consciously remind ourselves again that the past is in the past and all things are again possible. We must also reboot our commitment to be true to ourselves.*

- *Being open to new possibilities is kryptonite to our machinery.*

Committing to potentiality creates the opportunity to get what we want!

- *A victory for the soul is often experienced as a defeat for the ego.*

- *Vitality is a function of participation. The more you participate, the greater is your aliveness, so stop being merely a spectator!*

- *When you aren't participating as a player, then you are the one being played!*

- *Resisting saps vitality and causes emotional death.*

- *The more you participate in life, the more alive you are.*

- *The real joy in life comes from the process, not the result!*

- *The "blur" in our lives is a result of not making choices. We get a lot more power by just saying "Yes" or "No." When we say "Yes" or "No," the muddle or fog or bind goes away. We need to make choices in order to make a difference.*

- *You miss 100 percent of the shots you never take.*

Pause Your Machinery

- Take out the list you made at the end of chapter 1—of incidents that didn't work out the way you would have liked.

- Read the list over, comparing your first description of the incidents—which included your thoughts about it, how it made you feel, how you acted and reacted, as well as what the other people involved did or said—with your second description—which contained just the facts. See if you now feel that how you acted and reacted during any of these incidents was not the most constructive response to the situation and perhaps even sabotaged you from getting what you wanted.

- If you now feel your actions and reactions were self-defeating, can you see how you were acting on automatic pilot, following your programming?

- Can you see how, without realizing it at the time, the tale you told yourself about the situation programmed you so that you would have a negative experience similar to other negative experiences you had in the past?

- For each incident, describe the Organizing Principles—the beliefs you held about the world and your place in it—that you were operating under at the time that caused you to act as you did.

- For each incident, describe the character you played and how playing that character created the outcome you were unsatisfied with.

- Would you like to handle these situations differently today by interrupting your machinery and not allowing your programming to control you? If so, what actions could you employ to prevent repeating the same habitual response?

- Are you committed to staying in the present and not the past or the future?

NOTES

PREFACE

1. James Allen, *As a Man Thinketh* (New York: Tarcher/ Penguin, 2008).

CHAPTER 7

1. Leana Foster Melat in a conversation with the author.
2. C. G. Jung, *Collected Works of C. G. Jung*, Vol. 8 (Princeton, NJ: Princeton University Press, 1970) 200.
3. Leana Foster Melat, "The Mythical and Psychological Meaning of a Woman's Purse," Doctoral Dissertation. (Santa Barbara, CA: Pacific Graduate Institute for Depth Psychology, 2000) 85-86.
4. Leana Foster Melat in a conversation with the author.
5. C. G. Jung, *Collected Works of C. G. Jung*, Vol. 8 (Princeton, NJ: Princeton University Press, 1970) 204.
6. C. G. Jung, *Collected Works of C. G. Jung*, Vol. 6 (Princeton, NJ: Princeton University Press, 1971) 797.
7. Leana Foster Melat, "The Mythical and Psychological Meaning of a Woman's Purse," Doctoral Dissertation. (Santa Barbara, CA: Pacific Graduate Institute for Depth Psychology, 2000) 104. Readers interested in reading further about Jung on complexes should read C. G. Jung, *Collected Works of C. G. Jung*, Vol. 8, 3rd chapter, "Review of the Complex Theory." (Princeton, NJ: Princeton University Press, 1970).
8. C. G. Jung, *Collected Works of C. G. Jung*, Vol. 16 (Princeton, NJ: Princeton University Press, 1966) 179.
9. C. G. Jung, *Collected Works of C. G. Jung*, Vol. 7 (Princeton, NJ: Princeton University Press, 1967) 488.
10. Leana Foster Melat, "The Mythical and Psychological Meaning of a Woman's Purse," Doctoral Dissertation.

(Santa Barbara, CA: Pacific Graduate Institute for Depth Psychology, 2000) 88.

CHAPTER 10

1. C. G. Jung writes about the dark side throughout his works. For more information about the dark side, see particularly C. G. Jung, *Collected Works of C. G. Jung*, Vol. 6 (Princeton, NJ: Princeton University Press, 1971) and C. G. Jung, *Collected Works of C. G. Jung*, Vol. 9, Part 2 (Princeton, NJ: Princeton University Press, 1969).

2. C. G. Jung, *Collected Works of C. G. Jung*, Vol. 9, Part 2 (Princeton, NJ: Princeton University Press, 1969) 423.

3. Leana Foster Melat in a conversation with the author.

4. Ibid.

5. Ibid.

6. C. G. Jung, *Collected Works of C. G. Jung*, Vol. 13 (Princeton, NJ: Princeton University Press, 1968) 335.

CHAPTER 11

1. Talmud, Shabbat 31a.

CHAPTER 14

1. Leana Foster Melat in a conversation with the author.

2. Ibid.

3. Ibid.

4. Ibid.

5. Ibid.

6. Ibid.

7. Ibid.

8. Leana Foster Melat in a conversation with the author. For more information about Dr. Melat's exploration of complexes, see Leana Foster Melat, "The Mythical and Psychological Meaning of a Woman's Purse," Doctoral Dissertation. (Santa Barbara, CA: Pacific Graduate Institute for Depth Psychology, 2000). Readers interested in reading further about Jung on complexes should read C. G. Jung, *Collected Works of C. G. Jung*, Vol. 8, 3rd

chapter, "Review of the Complex Theory." (Princeton, NJ: Princeton University Press, 1970).

CHAPTER 17

1. Dr. Robin L. Kay in a conversation with the author.
2. Don Miguel Ruiz, *The Four Agreements* (San Rafael, CA: Amber-Allen Publishing, 1997).
3. Dalai Lama, *The Art of Living* (New York: Gramercy Books, 2005).

CHAPTER 18

1. Ramit Plushnick-Masti with Ramesh Santanam, "Professor whose 'Last Lecture' became best-seller, dies (+video)" New Zealand Herald (July 28, 2008), http://www.nzherald.co.nz/healthy-living/news/article.cfm?c_id=1501238&objectid=10523853&pnum=0.

Index

A

activated, 28–30, 56, 62, 64, 66, 72, 77–79, 99, 126, 142, 151

anxiety, 4–5, 19, 27, 31, 55, 62, 68, 108, 124, 138, 142, 168–169, 173

archetypes
    Father, 63
    in the collective unconscious, 95
    Mother, 63

authentic being, 126, 137, 150, 161, 164. *See also* authentic self

authentic self, 95–96, 138. *See also* authentic being

automatic pilot, 28–30, 57, 73, 86, 111, 117, 119, 120, 124, 138,182. *See also* manual

automatics, 29

awkward pain, 108, 113. *See also* unfamiliar pain; familiar pain

B

beingness, 12–13, 18, 30

blank slate, 51

blind men and the elephant, 52

breathing exercise, 168–169

Buddhist philosophy, 162

C

coherent autobiographical narrative, 158

collective unconscious, 63, 95. *See also* personal unconscious

complex, definition of, 61

core issues, 50–51, 141. *See also* core story

core story, 53, 56, 83. *See also* core issues

critic, 167, 171, 175

cynicism, 43, 126, 136, 143, 160

D

Dalai Lama, 173

dark side, 95–103, 108, 137, 152, 172. *See also* shadow side

K

Kay, Dr. Robin L., iii, 25, 157
keeping a journal, 169–173

L

lessons about relationships. *See* relationships
Levine, Rabbi Dr. Ron, iii, 112
libido, 67–68

M

machinery, definition of, 13
manual, 27, 86, 111, 112, 120, 124. *See also* automatic pilot
Melat, Dr. Leana, iii, 61–62, 65, 67–68, 129–134, 136–137
memory, 27, 40, 54, 100, 130, 133–134
mindfulness, 14, 24, 77, 167
misinterpretation, 27, 28, 31, 124, 142
Mother archetype, 63. *See also* archetypes

P

pain, our machinery's response to, 56–58
patterns of behavior, 5, 23–24, 53, 61, 73, 85–86, 90, 129, 131,142
Pausch, Randy, 178–179
pause your machinery, 14–15, 20, 31–32, 40–41, 74, 82, 89, 99–100, 120, 124, 135, 142–143, 182–183
pebble-in-the-shoe problems, 50
persona, 72–73, 75–76, 78 97, 176
personal unconscious, 95. *See also* collective unconscious
personality DNA, 41
prison cell, freeing ourselves from, 58
programming, definition of, 13

R

relationships, 4, 7, 18, 26, 49, 50, 53, 56–57, 88–89, 100–101, 109,113, 119, 131, 135, 142–143, 145–153, 162, 171, 176, 179 resistance, 125, 136, 138

ruptures, of emotional attachment to parent, 25, 26. *See also* trauma, emotional

S
self-defeating cycle, 118

set way of presenting ourselves, 76, 78, 83, 88, 118, 138, 170, 176

shadow side, 98, 136. *See also* dark side

stress, 2, 4, 19, 27, 32, 49, 55, 62, 63, 65, 91

T
talk therapy, 50

trauma, emotional, 23, 24, 25–26, 54, 62, 75, 157–158

U
unfamiliar pain, 58, 118–119. *See also* familiar pain; awkward pain

universal consciousness, 173

W
woolly mammoth, 13, 19, 24, 30, 63, 72, 75, 78–79

Z
Zen, 177